The *Baby* and the *Bathwater*

Aspiration and Reality in the Life of the Church

ROBERT J. SUDERMAN
ILLUSTRATION BY RAY DIRKS

The Baby and the Bathwater
Copyright © 2021 by Robert J. Suderman

All biblical references are taken from the
New Revised Standard Version.

The wood-etching on the cover was done in 1512
c.e. The name of the artist is unknown.

This book is available at all the usual commercial
outlets. It is also available at the Mennonite
Church Canada resource centre Common Word
www.commonword.ca/go/2320 or info@commonword.ca

All rights reserved. No part of this publication may be
reproduced, distributed, or transmitted in any form or by
any means, including photocopying, recording, or other
electronic or mechanical methods, without the prior
written permission of the author, except in the case of
brief quotations embodied in critical reviews and certain
other non-commercial uses permitted by copyright law.

Tellwell Talent
www.tellwell.ca

ISBN
978-0-2288-5093-9 (Paperback)

Table of Contents

Dedication v
Acknowledgements vii
Foreword...ix
Prologue... xiii
Introduction xvii

Wheat and Weeds: Coexistence as Vocation............................. 1
Advancing toward the End Is Going Back to the Beginning 7
The Strategic Plan: Moving from There to Here
    or From Here to There 13
96 Images – but Who's Counting... 21
A Closer Look at Ekklesia (Church) 27
The Church as a Branch Entwined with the Vine..................... 37
The Church as Teacher 51
A Community of Hope... 61

Appendix 69
Afterwords 77
Other Books Published.. 87
What Others Are Saying 89
About the Author 97
About the Illustrator 99

Dedication

This booklet is dedicated to the innumerable, yet largely invisible, mentors, practitioners, and leaders from at home and around the globe who have helped to inspire and shape my understandings of the biblical text and the vocation of the church within it.

You have taught me, engaged me in conversation, helped me understand your context, and granted me the privilege of watching your leadership. You have demonstrated the relevance of Scripture and inspired me with your commitment and passion for the church. You have been a blessing to me and to my family.

Acknowledgements

I wish to thank my wife, Irene, and our family for their continued encouragement, support, and helpful advice. Your solidarity in a project such as this is incalculable.

I also thank Doug Klassen and Katie Doke Sawatzky from Mennonite Church Canada. Their support, in multiple ways, has been definitive in moving this project along. I also thank Doug for the insightful and energizing Foreword he has written for the book. Thank you for your trust and your commitment to making this project happen.

I want to thank Ray Dirks – friend, colleague, and superb artist – for agreeing to illustrate the chapters of this book. Ray brings his extensive creativity and insight to say things via his drawings that I cannot say with words. His work enriches the book dramatically.

I want to thank the three persons who were willing to add depth, experience, and insight to the text. Cynthia Peacock has been a long-time colleague in Mennonite World Conference. We have shared our contexts together on multiple occasions. Janet Plenert has been a close working colleague in Mennonite Church Canada and in Mennonite World Conference for many years. She has taught me the value of story in communication and has always found ways of implementing what may appear to be lofty ideas. Moses Falco is a young pastor in Winnipeg. He is asking some of the very same questions that have been on my mind for decades. I appreciate what he refers to as "wrestling." May we continue to do so.

I want to thank the leaders from my own denomination as well as those sharing insightful endorsements from around the globe and from a rich diversity of ecumenical backgrounds. Your solidarity in a common cause has encouraged me greatly. I trust, as some have indicated, that this modest work may be useful in a wide range of ecumenical settings where the vocation of the church is on our agendas.

I want to thank the publishing team from Tellwell Talent. This includes the consultant Scott Lunn, project manager Redjell Arcillas, cover design Benjamin Mosquera, interior design Joseph Apuhin, copy editor and proofreader Jean Rath. Your fine and professional work is evident on every page.

Finally, my thanks to God and to the biblical writers for exposing us to such an amazing and inspiring vision in which normal people like ourselves, in diverse historical circumstances, can together function as agents for God's giant and cosmic restoration project.

Foreword

In October 1993, I joined several other youth ministers for a two-week learning tour to Colombia, South America. The purpose of the trip was to expose young church leaders to the Colombian Mennonite Church in the hopes of learning from them and establishing lasting church relationships.

Our group arrived in Bogotá, then declared to be one of the most violent cities in the world. At the time, it was experiencing an average 16 violent deaths per day, only a tiny percentage of which were ever investigated. Soldiers with machine guns lined the walls of the airport.

Within a day or two we arrived at the home of Robert (Jack) and Irene Suderman. I knew their son Bryan and looked forward to meeting his parents. We were generously and joyfully welcomed. Irene has a way of making everyone feel like beloved family. After some wonderful food, including Colombian fruit, which is a whole new level of taste, we sat in a circle to talk about Jack's favourite subject – the church.

Jack told us about his time teaching at a seminary in Bolivia. There, under dictatorship, he and others were forbidden to teach the Sermon on the Mount (Matthew 5-7) because the words of Jesus contain ideas that threatened the oppressive power structures of the country. Not deterred, Jack taught the students the reasons why he couldn't teach them about the Sermon on the Mount.

Then he began to tell us about the project of establishing a Mennonite seminary in Colombia that he and other leaders were working on. As he spoke, we heard a loud "Boom!" Jack kept talking. The rest of us began looking out the corner of our eyes at each other. Seeing that we were distracted, Jack paused to say, "That was probably just a bomb going off at the university across the street. So, as I was saying…"

Looking momentarily at Irene and then Jack, I thought, "Who are these people?!?" They are living in a country wracked with violence from a decades-long struggle between government and guerrilla groups fuelled by drug trafficking; they are living in a city where you are told not to run down a sidewalk because the people around you will think that someone is going to get shot; they are working in a church where a prominent church leader had been gunned down and the leader of the justice and peace arm was recently evacuated to the USA because his name appeared in published death-threat lists; they are visiting some congregations where ushers keep their eyes open for kidnappers lurking outside. And I? I had just come from a series of church meetings back home where members were strongly objecting to the new hymnal because it contained 25 more unison songs than the old one! Lord, have mercy!

That night in the Suderman home, and the days that followed, changed my life. I encountered more people like Jack and Irene – disciples of Jesus who not only spoke about the Sermon on the Mount but lived the dreams and dangers of it day after day.

When the Suderman's returned to Canada, Jack began his work as an executive staff member of what later would become Mennonite Church Canada. In his writing, teaching, and preaching, Jack became to Mennonite Church Canada what Lesslie Newbigin was to the broader Christian church. Newbigin, upon his return to Great Britain from years in India, wrote: "It is surely a fact of inexhaustible significance that what our Lord left behind Him was not a book . . . but a visible community."

Amid the impact of fundamentalist and revivalist preaching that had left its mark on Mennonites, Jack led a quest to recover an understanding of "the people of God" (1 Peter 2:9-10) as God's chosen vehicle for proclaiming healing and hope for the world, and to be faithful to that call in our time.

While the counsel of some church consultants was to "just go out and do it," thereby discouraging any effort to profoundly understand the biblical vision of peoplehood, Jack and Irene had been "living it" in South America. How could this be translated to Canadian culture?

Figuratively speaking, Jack, like the prophet Habakkuk, stood on the rampart of a walled-in western church and waited for God to speak. God did speak. "Write the vision; Make it plain…" (Habakkuk 2:2).

The Face of Mennonite Mission in the 21st Century followed. This series of articles was a "word" to the Mennonite Church in Canada. As with every word, there was resistance. What is this new buzz word… missional?

But through persistence and grace, the calling and encouragement of young leaders, and the continued fostering of connections with the global church, the vision caught. While there is still a long journey ahead for the western church, and though it may be some years yet before the church is freed from the bonds of Christendom, the vision is before us. It is biblical, historical, and intercultural, and it is filled with eschatological hope.

This little book is Jack's magnum opus, but made plain. Each chapter could be expanded into a lengthy thesis, but that is not what is needed at this time.

If you are a student who sees the church becoming irrelevant in the midst of a growing secularism in Canada; if you are a pastor that has been discouraged by the petty disagreements that go on in your community; if you are a church leader – local, regional or nationwide – who is concerned about what the church is going to look like on the other side of COVID-19, don't throw the baby out with the bathwater. Instead, read, study, struggle with, and devour this book with

Ezekiel-like dedication (Ezekiel 3), and you will discover a sweet word for our time.

This book won't give you clever new techniques to engage a post-COVID world, but it will re-ground you in what God has been doing throughout human history, that is, empowering a people – a community of faith – to proclaim in word and deed a message of healing and hope for all of creation.

- Rev. Doug Klassen, Executive Minister, Mennonite Church Canada

Prologue

Our seminary experiences in the early 1970s fanned a spark of interest in understanding the church into red-hot flames. It was there that I first sensed a growing gap between our Christian doctrines and their resulting ethics; I also sensed the increased marginalization of significant ecclesiology, or "peoplehood" as I prefer to speak of it. The priorities of faith that have become prevalent and increasingly dominant over the decades, by and large, do not include the church as an essential component.

I should modify that statement. When I say "the church," I am talking here about functional – both personal and organizational – understandings and expressions of faith, not the impressive textbooks of doctrine, systematic theological tomes, and liturgical practices. Conversion and salvation, it seems, can be explained without the church. Peace-making and justice-activism also don't seem to need it. Community development work gets along just fine without close attention to the church as part of its strategy. Even evangelism and discipleship have marginalized the church to some outer rim. Ecclesiology – the nature and vocation of the church – receives some formal lip service in theological and churchly seminary circles, but it has long since been marginalized as a significant player in the everyday lives of individual Christians, as well as in church-based organizations and church programs and as a focus that really matters.

I have spent much of my academic and church-leadership time decrying this rapid decline of the centrality of ecclesiology in the theological frameworks we have built. But I have spent even more time attempting to articulate a compelling, biblical case for the centrality of the church in our Christian understandings and life. More recently, some have encouraged (pushed) me to prepare a written summary of these understandings. This manuscript is my effort to do so.

This manuscript should be seen as a summary. It does not include all the documentation that would be helpful. It is the fruit of at least 50 years of focus on questions of the role of the church in our understanding of Christian discipleship.

As such, I trust it can be helpful.

Dr. Robert J. Suderman
New Hamburg, Ontario
June, 2021

Introduction

"Don't throw out the baby with the bathwater."[1]

I have used this saying to speak to some who are disgusted with the witness of the church in history and today, and who want to disregard its importance. God knows: there are more than enough reasons to be disgusted and discouraged. The church has not lived up to its noble vocation. Throughout its checkered history, it has aided and abetted oppression, injustice, and inequality in every way imaginable. We must begin by acknowledging that. I don't think detail is needed here.

Yet, critique of the church is possible only if we assume that criteria for measurement exist. Without common criteria, we cannot be sure whether we are doing well or poorly. So that, then, is the first question: What are the criteria that tell us that the church has failed? And if, indeed, the church has failed, what then? Should we align the church more closely with the criteria that we use to measure it? Or do we adjust the criteria to justify the inadequacy of the church thus making failure the new norm? I'm afraid that for some, the answer is to keep adjusting the criteria or to throw them away altogether. Doing so, however, does not improve the witness of the church. It only accommodates us more easily to an unfaithful status quo. Lived reality then becomes our passion and our guiding star – our grasp exceeds our reach, and heaven is no longer needed (adapted from poet Robert Browning).

---

[1] Earliest record of this phrase comes from *Narrenbeschwörung* (*Appeal to Fools*) by Thomas Murner, a Franciscan priest, in 1512 c.e. Murner was a priest, theologian, and satirist. It was accompanied by the wood-etching used on the cover. The identity of the artist is unknown.

The adage about the baby and the bathwater, actually, has a rich history. It is first cited in 1512 c.e. in the satirical writings of Thomas Murner, a Franciscan priest. Murner was a poet, theologian, and satirist. He lived and wrote before and during the time of the Protestant Reformation (1475-1537 c.e.). He was born 30 km from Strasbourg, France, and later lived in Strasbourg during the 1520s. He used his significant wit and brilliance to attack the efforts of Martin Luther, Ulrich Zwingli, and the entire Reformation project. He participated with Dr. Eck in the well-known disputation against Luther in Baden, in May 1526.

In his book *Appeal to Fools* (1512 c.e.), Murner uses the phrase (in German): "*das kind ausschütten mit dem bad*" (the child thrown out with the bath). In the book, he satirizes some of what is happening in the social, political, and religious context of the time. Clergy, princes, knights, and deceitful lawyers do not escape his satirical wit as he exposes – through satire – the plight of the German peasants.

After 1517, Murner also turned his sights on the Reformation and the Reformers. He was especially interested in how the Reformers were adjusting the dominant understandings of church. Given his location in Strasbourg, and given his focus on Zwingli, one must assume that he would have been aware of the Anabaptists as well. I want to appropriate this saying now to help us think again about the nature and vocation of the church in light of 21st century realities. We too are in a moment of significant reformation – perhaps as important or more so than the one in the 16th century. The image of the baby and the bathwater is, again, relevant for us.

I am fully aware of the irony that I am now using this phrase to defend some of what he critiqued. Namely, I am suggesting that the Reformation efforts to recover a biblical vision for the church are again as urgent today as they were in the 16th century. Murner defended the then existing church in the face of pressures for change. I am using this phrase to critique the erosion of ecclesiology in the existing church, thus advocating for something more robust in our understandings of the centrality of the church. Nevertheless, the phrase is helpful in each context.

Throwing out the baby with the bathwater points to human tendencies to let go of what is good in our zeal to deal with what is bad. We get rid of both. Or sometimes we eliminate what is essential and retain what is less so. Not only have we then hung on to the bad, we have eliminated the good which could make the bad less bad.

I am aware that by using language such as "good" and "bad" I am presuming that we have the capacity to discern between the two. This, in our context, is already provocative. The same is true for "baby" and "bathwater." It assumes that, somehow, we can tell the difference or that the two are separable. Again, criteria are called for if, indeed, the process is to be legitimate.

In the reflections that follow, I propose to examine, in as simple a way as I can, the biblical trajectory and wisdom undergirding the nature and vocation of the church. I trust that we can draw a distinction between "simple" and "simplistic." The profound integrity of the biblical call to function in the world as the people of God is really quite simple, yet it continues to be very penetrating.

Wheat and Weeds: Coexistence as Vocation

Jesus highlights the vocation of the church and addresses the issue of the baby and bathwater in his parable about the weeds and the wheat (Mt. 13:24-43). Let's take a closer look.

Jesus is trying to illustrate how the "kingdom[2] of heaven" functions amid enemies and evil. It is a simple story. A landowner goes out to plant good seeds in the ground and then goes to bed. While he is sleeping, an enemy comes and sows weeds among the good wheat seeds. When the wheat grows, the weeds grow with it. The servants are dumbfounded: Where did these weeds come from? We thought you had good seed. Jesus responds: The seeds were good, but an enemy came and sowed weeds among the good seeds. The servants ask: Should we go and pull out all the weeds of the enemy? Jesus says no. Let them both grow together because by pulling out the weeds you may also pull out the

---

[2] A brief word about the use of "kingdom" is in order here. I am aware that this word is controversial. It seems to point to territory rather than condition; it is a term of power and can be inferred to be oppressive and hierarchical; it is masculine and can be used to undergird patriarchy. Some translations have opted for other words. I understand the word – fundamentally – to mean "authority." The authority of God is making itself known anew in the world. I have indicated that all quotations used in this book are taken from the New Revised Standard Version of the Bible. That translation continues to use the word "kingdom," and for this reason I will use it, although by no means do I use it exclusively. The careful reader will note many other words and images also used as partial synonyms and modifiers of "kingdom." I trust we will see that the New Testament's use of the word is not designed to be either territorial, hierarchical, oppressive, or patriarchal.

roots of the wheat. At the time of harvest the reapers will separate the weeds and the wheat.

The disciples are perplexed. After the crowds are gone, they ask Jesus to clarify what he meant. Jesus carefully identifies the components of the story. The sower is the Son of Man; the field is the world; the good seed are the children of the kingdom; the weeds are the children of the evil one; the enemy is the evil one; the reapers are the angels; the harvest is the end of time.

How can wheat and weeds cohabit the same territory? Many have followed Chrysostom's suggestion that this parable speaks to the issue of discipline in the church, i.e., heresy.[3] I don't think it does. Jesus explains that the "field is the world," it is not the church. The question is not how do the "children of the kingdom" live with those who have gone astray. The point is that there is a distinction between the "children of the kingdom" and the "world"; between the seeds of the sower and the seeds of the evil one; between the wheat and the weeds. The issue at hand is not how to discipline our own but how to live in the same world as those who are not "children of the kingdom." This parable does not speak to the question of church discipline; it speaks to the question of the relationship between "children of the kingdom" and "children of the evil one."

Is it the responsibility of the "children of the kingdom" to uproot the evil of the world with the use of force? Jesus' answer is "No." The wheat and the weeds will cohabit the same world. The wheat continues to be wheat; the weeds continue to be weeds. The wheat does not do violence to the

---

[3] John Chrysostom's homily on Matthew 13: "But what means, 'Lest ye root up the wheat with them?' Either He means this, If ye are to take up arms, and to kill the heretics, many of the saints also must needs be overthrown with them; or that of the very tares it is likely that many may change and become wheat. If therefore ye root them up beforehand, ye injure that which is to become wheat, slaying some, in whom there is yet room for change and improvement. He doth not therefore forbid our checking heretics, and stopping their mouths, and taking away their freedom of speech, and breaking up their assemblies and confederacies, but our killing and slaying them."

weeds lest, in so doing, the wheat is coopted by the mechanisms of the weeds to achieve its ends, thus destroying both. Neither does the wheat attempt to graft the weeds into its own stalk so that the two become one. Rather, the wheat and the weeds simply need to grow together in the same world. If separation is needed, that is not the responsibility of the "children of the kingdom." The time will come when this is done. It will be done by the angels.

In the Gospel of Matthew, both John the Baptist and Jesus have already announced that "the kingdom of heaven has come near" (Mt. 3:2; 4:17). Jesus then teaches what this means. The term "kingdom of heaven" appears five times in the Beatitudes and the Sermon on the Mount, and is used another 25 times in the Gospel. What is going on? Two key elements are evident. One is Jesus' conviction that God's kingdom has become present in some new and unprecedented way. The other is that immediately following his announcement of the kingdom coming, Jesus begins to gather disciples whose job it is to learn to live in the world but within this new reality of the kingdom's presence (Mt. 4:18-22). In the parable of the wheat and the weeds, this community is referred to as "children of the kingdom." These "children" function as seeds. Jesus' announcement of the coming kingdom, and the organizational effort to create communities of "children of the kingdom," are entirely inseparable. The vocation of this new kingdom community is to be wheat among the weeds – to grow up together.

This parable could suggest several options. First, the disciples consider the possibility of removing the weeds to keep the wheat pure. Jesus says no: we do not maintain purity in the wheat by inflicting violence on the weeds. Indeed, the opposite would happen: the integrity of the wheat would also be implicated, and it would disappear along with the weeds – the baby would be thrown out with the bathwater. The wheat is designed to live among the weeds – the children of the kingdom need to grow up alongside the evil seeds of the world.

Second, what if the wheat would graft itself into the weeds or the weeds into the wheat? Would this not resolve the issue? This too is not what

Jesus has in mind. In the grafting process, the wheat would no longer be all it is designed to be. The children of the kingdom would, in some way, become the children of the evil one too. They would lose their identity.

Stanley Hauerwas, noted theologian, has put it this way: "… the first task of the church is not to make the world more just. Rather the first task of the church is to make the world the world."[4]

So Jesus reiterates his preferred option: Allow the wheat and the weeds to grow up together (13:30). I suspect this option is meant to function in two ways: one, the wheat (the presence of the kingdom in the world) maintains its own integrity even among the evil surrounding it; two, the weeds need to see and experience an alternative to evil. We don't need a demonstration plot when all the surrounding plots are excelling equally. We do need it when the other plots are strangled with weeds. The "children of the kingdom" in this parable are to function as demonstration plots among the weeds. They are to be visible and tangible signs of the coming of the kingdom of heaven. As Chrysostom points out, the weeds do need an opportunity to change, and they do need to see that change is possible. This demonstration of the potential for transformation is, in a nutshell, the vocation of the church – the children of the kingdom.

---

[4] Stanley Hauerwas, "Why Bonhoeffer matters: The challenge for Christian ministry at the end of Christendom" (ABC Religion and Ethics, July 14, 2017)

Advancing toward the End Is Going Back to the Beginning

The emerging presence of the kingdom of heaven/God is the primary passion of Jesus' teaching and ministry. "Kingdom of heaven" appears 29 times in Matthew, along with five references to the "kingdom of God" and 15 references to "kingdom." In Mark's Gospel, there are 16 references to kingdom, and in Luke, we find 43 references.

The coming and presence of the kingdom of God is the undergirding framework of Jesus' understanding of gospel. Indeed, when Jesus succinctly defines the "good news," he makes no reference to himself. He refers only to the approach of the kingdom as the fulfillment of God's timing (*kairos*) (cf. Mark 1:15).

In each of the synoptic Gospels, Jesus begins and ends his teaching ministry by framing everything in terms of the coming kingdom (cf. Matthew 4:17, 25:1; Mark 1:15, 14:25; Luke 4:43, 22:18). In the previous chapter, we noted that it is the guiding vocation of the children of the kingdom to be the presence of the kingdom among the weeds of the world. They are to be signs that an alternative kingdom is possible and already present. The world does not need to remain the way it is.

We can walk through the Gospels and pick up fragments of what it means that the kingdom is emerging. There is, first and foremost, the re-creation of a people of the kingdom. In each of the Gospels, this is the very first action of Jesus after revealing that the emerging kingdom is his social, political, spiritual, and personal platform. That is the key;

it is foundational to everything else. Jesus understands the coming of the kingdom to be a restoration of peoplehood. On this foundation, there can be love of enemies, discernment of spiritual gifts, worship, discipleship, accountability, ethical guidance, restored relationships, prophetic action, and the reconciliation of everything. In a word, there can be a new creation and a new humanity, and the renewed community is called to be a sign of this new potential.

Yet, such a big, inspiring thrust needs a clear, compelling, and encyclopedic picture of what the vision really is. Fragments and excerpts are not good enough. Four personal anecdotes come to mind.

In Bogotá, Colombia, I was slated to give an address to an ecumenical group of political activists. The theme was "Biblical Foundations for Peace." One of the participants spoke to me before I began, hoping, I think, to rightly impress me with his pre-knowledge of peace issues in Colombia. He said: "So what kind of peace are you going to be talking about? Social, political, internal, ecological, or spiritual?" I replied: "Yes."

On another occasion, I was to speak to students and faculty at an evangelical university in Indonesia. Again, the theme was "The Social Understanding of Peace." Knowing that my invitation was a direct result of me being Mennonite, a historic peace church, I used the teachings, ministry, and life of Jesus as a model for what biblical peace is and what it is not. The Dean of the university had prepared a response to my paper. He thanked me for the address and then added: "I suppose it would have been only fair to let you know that here we decided several years ago that the ethic and example of Jesus are not really relevant for the situation of interfaith tensions that we are facing in Indonesia."

A third example comes from Cuba. Again, I was invited to address students and faculty at the most prestigious protestant seminary in Cuba on the theme of "The Politics of Jesus and Its Relevance Today." Again I made my presentation, and the President of the seminary responded: "Thank you for your presentation. But it really is an assortment of hand-picked biblical verses that happen to suit your preferences, not to mention those of your denomination. It's not realistic for our revolutionary context."

A fourth example comes from India. I was invited by the Peace Department of an evangelical seminary to make a presentation about "Our Responsibility for Peace." Again, I focused my comments on the biblical story. A senior student responded: "In our context we cannot use any language or concepts referring to the Bible, God, Jesus, Holy Spirit, or the church. All of this has failed. We must find an alternative Christian framework." He was passionately supported by one of his professors.

Why do I reveal these failures to communicate well? I think the four have some things in common. Each one is searching for an overarching, foolproof, compelling argument that leaves no stone unturned. Given that each of the four were Christian, evangelical contexts, I thought it was safe to use the example of Jesus as a sufficient foundation. In each case, according to authoritative voices in the audience, I was wrong. Furthermore, each response was assuming that criteria must exist whereby Christian faithfulness can be measured. Vague, hazy, and partial focuses would not do. I thought I had done that within the limitations of the time I was allotted, but apparently they didn't see it.

What these folks were looking for is legitimate. The vision of "good news" must be encompassing enough to speak to the daily struggles of multiple contexts. If it doesn't speak to my struggle, it is not "good news" for me. The Paul of Ephesians indicates that in the "fullness of time" God's plan is "to gather up all things in him, things in heaven and things on earth" (1:10). The three-fold repetition of "things," is a way of underlining that nothing will be left out. Everything will be "gathered up" (ἀνακεφαλαιώσασθαι), reconciled, united, and included in one framework. Yet even this grand promise does not provide details. How does this actually look? What is it like?

It seems that the Christian traditions that framed the biblical canon anticipated these questions and concerns. The Bible begins and ends with remarkable visions of how things are meant to be. We refer to the beginning as the Garden of Eden and the end as the New Jerusalem. These have striking similarities.

Both Eden and the New Jerusalem are visions of the world, our world, and how it could be. They are both environmentally holistic, contemplating planets, stars, water, air, soil, vegetation, animals, birds, and humans. They both celebrate the diversity present in God's creation. The vision is cosmic. As indicated in Ephesians, it is the reconciliation of all things in heaven and on earth (1:10). It could not be bigger.

Both Eden and the New Jerusalem are dedicated to life. Both have rivers that flow out to nourish the needs of the living things. Both assign human beings significant responsibilities to maintain the integrity of what is; we may call this stewardship, or justice. Both call on humanity to serve the intentions of what is there. In both, preserving the integrity of what is means that there are certain limitations to what can happen. While the gates are always open to the New Jerusalem, nothing impure can enter. Suffering and pain are not included. Neither is death. Most of all, in both, it is the authority of God that governs because these are the conditions that God wants for all of creation. God's intentions are fulfilled, and the world submits wholly to the will of God. This is the best definition we have of the "kingdom of God." It is not so much an exact location than a condition of life under the authority of God.

In summary, both Eden and the New Jerusalem paint pictures of peace, harmony, justice, equality, cooperation, integrity, respect for diversity, environmental balance, and much more. They are comprehensive pictures of what has been, what can be, and what will be. Or, if this sounds too delusory, they are images of what God's intentions have been, are, and will be. They include the yearnings for comprehensive peace in Colombia, the reconciliation of interfaith tensions in Indonesia, the passionate hopes of the revolution in Cuba, and the undoing of unjust conditions of oppression aimed at the Dalit – the untouchables – in India.

When Jesus announces that the coming of the kingdom of God is his platform for action, i.e., the Gospel, he has in mind a restoration of the universe with the scope of Eden and the New Jerusalem. It is not a call to save us from the evils of the world, but a call to reconcile the world to what it can be. It is a vocation to be wheat among the weeds, hoping that the weeds can be transformed without damaging the identity of the wheat. It is a vocation of growing together and granting God the prerogative of navigating the harvest.

The Strategic Plan: Moving from There to Here or From Here to There

If Eden and the New Jerusalem are indeed the paradigms that illustrate God's dream for the world, then we have a problem. Or maybe, then God has a problem. It doesn't take much to realize that the creation – our world – is neither the way it was intended to be nor what it is meant to become. Turn on the television news, read a newspaper, take a walk around town, read some history books, listen to some songs, look at expressions of art, or search your own soul: evidence of Eden or the New Jerusalem is not the most obvious. We see violence and injustice, inequality and marginalization, lies and scams, quarrels and misunderstandings, revenge and oppression, greed and competition, contamination and pollution.

The Bible uses a 3-letter word (in English) to describe all this. It is sin. Wolfhart Pannenberg, a German theologian, has described sin as searching for life at fountains that are not life-giving. I like that definition; it describes what is happening all around and within us. It affirms that we all yearn for life; indeed, the essence of life itself is a persistent search for life. Once we no longer search for life, we are dead. The definition also suggests that we search for life at sources that are not life-giving. The answer to sin is not to stop searching for life; it is to search in places that are truly life-generating. The use of violence, ironically, is a search for life. But it is a strategy that is ultimately destructive. Greed is a search for life, but it too destroys rather than restores. The reality of sin can be personal, communal, and systemic. It can be embedded in our hearts, our traditions, our habits and routines, our culture, our religious expression, our structures, our politics, and in morality, ethics, and actions. It is pervasive.

Two elements of being human jump into sight. One is humanity's common search for life. The other is humanity's need to discover the sources that generate life. These things bind us all together, everywhere, all the time. But there is a third element. While humanity searches for the sources where life in its fullness can be found, there is no consensus on what the sources are. A lack of consensus, however, does not mean that there is a lack of ideas. These abound – systemically, personally, religiously, socially, and politically.

At a macro level, for example, capitalism, socialism, and communism are all searching for life with a common assumption that it can best be found at the fountain of economics and material sustenance. Democracy, dictatorship, and oligarchy are searching for life at a common fountain, namely, that communally imposed social obligations will generate the life we seek.

At a micro level, relationships, friendships, and marriage are attempts to search for life, each one drinking at the fountain of our desire for community. Status, glamour, and rank are life-seeking mechanisms nurtured by fountains serving up personal power and prestige.

But as we walk the streets and interact with our world, there are also signs of Eden and the New Jerusalem – not in their full glory, but leaning in the right direction. These signs are macro and micro, personal and systemic. Generosity is evident, both spontaneous and structured. Hospitality is offered even at significant personal risk. There are efforts to implement justice, to structure equality, and to ensure compassion. Love is offered and received. Forgiveness is sought and granted. Lives are voluntarily sacrificed for the sake of others. Prejudice is confronted, racism is addressed, power is shared. Relationships are reconciled, acts of kindness are offered, lives are transformed. In other words, there is significant evidence of life sought at fountains that nurture life.

So what is God's strategy to get the world back on its intended track? The biblical canon indicates that we had Eden but then lost it, and now we are on the road to the New Jerusalem. But how? What are the key tools for the journey? What is the strategic plan?

These are questions we want to investigate in the next chapters. But we need to provide a framework here. I will mention only two ingredients for the biblical dream of the restoration of creation.

The first indispensable ingredient is people. This journey from the mountain-top of Eden through the valley of disruption to the plateau of reconciliation will involve people. Yes, God may choose, at points, to work through thunder, floods, manna, burning bushes, famine, exile, angels, and miracles. But all of these are sub-initiatives intended to impact the experiences and decisions of people.

From Adam and Eve, called to tend and serve the garden, to the dispersion of languages of those tempted by their own images at Babel, to the covenant with Abram and Sarah, called in their old age to nurture a family of blessing for others, God's chosen vehicle is people.

From the search for the food of Joseph's Egypt, to the call of Moses from the burning bush, to the miracle of the liberation of Israel from the cruelty of the Egyptian pharaohs, the focus is on the formation of people.

From the covenant and protection of the 40 years of wilderness wanderings, to the entrance into the promised land, God is creating a people of *torah* and *khokhma* – law and wisdom.

From the struggle of regional, tribal suzerainties to the misguided glory days of monarchies, God is forging a peoplehood of identity and purpose.

From the humiliation and devastation of exile to the new attempt at rebuilding the city, God is keeping faith with a covenanted people.

From the succession of conquests by Egyptian, Assyrian, Babylonian, Persian, Greek, and Roman empires to the tenacious survival within marginalization, God keeps shaping and nourishing an identity of people with a special vocation.

From temple to synagogue to people of the Way, God accompanies and blesses.

From the misconceived glories of violent kingship to the self-identity of suffering servanthood, God infuses wisdom and understanding into messianic peoplehood.

From a birth in a manger in Bethlehem to a cross in Jerusalem, God calls shepherds, fisherfolk, and zealots together to be children of the Kingdom.

With the power of resurrection from the dead, God creates a new community of life over death.

The names and experiences change, but the common denominator remains constant. God has chosen to put God's project for restoration of the world into the hands of people. This may sound too simplistic. It is not. It is indeed such a dominant presupposition that too often we do not dwell on it long enough to allow the profound nature of this truth to sink in.

This assumption has a sub-point. If the primary ingredient is people and peoplehood, it means that God has chosen to work through human history because humans are historical and not eternal beings. God's stage of action and God's strategic plan will, by necessity, be historical. Both Eden and the New Jerusalem are located on earth, in the world, amid the history of people. God's dream does not annihilate human history; it heals it. God's plan does not ignore or marginalize history; it brings it into a reconciled focus.

None of the biblically reported efforts of peoplehood formation are perfect. They all demonstrate the wheat and the weeds growing together.

Indeed, they witness to repeated realities of weeds being grafted into the wheat itself, and wheat grafted into the weeds. It is an historical process until harvest. The biblical canon itself is witness to God's serious commitment to work through human history. We have no original manuscripts available to us. What is available are copies of copies, all of them revealing significant shifts and changes. It is not that we are at the mercy of history; history itself is at the mercy of God's loving patience in revealing and implementing the intended purposes.

The second ingredient for God's restoration project is that it will happen with and under the authority of God's wisdom for the healing of history. This authority is described most often as the "kingdom of God." It is a realm in which the wisdom of God reigns. The strategic plan is a partnership between historical peoplehood and the reign of divine wisdom. The essence of this partnership is not grafting humanity into divinity or divinity into humanity, thus changing the nature of both. In this partnership of historical peoplehood and divine authority, we do not become little gods, nor does God become a little human.

The essence of this partnership is incarnation (literally "en-fleshing"). "And the Word became flesh and lived [tabernacled] among [or within] us" (John 1:14). The "Word," (*logos*) in John's prologue is a reference to the *torah* and *khokhma* (law and wisdom) of God. It is "enfleshed" in humanity. And we became capable of "beholding its glory." God's authority and wisdom can live in the flesh of human history, and in so doing human history lives in the light of God.

We do not do justice to the biblical record if we limit the hope for "incarnation" to the coming of Jesus into the world. The hope for incarnation is already present in the Genesis accounts of creating humanity in the "image" of God. It is present in Isaiah's vision of the people of God as a "suffering servant." It is present in the Fourth Gospel's hope that "they may be one, as we are one, I in them and you in me…" (John 17:22-23). It is present in the Ephesians description of the church as the "body" with the "fullness of him [God] who fills all in all" (Eph.

1:23). Incarnation always was and continues to be the strategy of God in fulfilling the intended purpose of creation.

In summary, the strategic plan of God calls for a historic peoplehood living under the authority of God, revealing in flesh the wisdom and law of God for creation. This peoplehood will serve as wheat among the weeds. It will be a sign that the reign of God's wisdom is already present. It will be the parabolic presence of what is to come – if we have eyes to see it and ears to hear it. God's hope is that peoplehood living within the framework of God's authority will move from Eden to the New Jerusalem.

96 Images – but Who's Counting

As indicated above, these reflections are attempting to trace the biblical trajectory and wisdom undergirding the nature and vocation of the church. We are almost ready to use the word "church" more substantively, but not quite yet. Experience has taught me that in some contemporary circles the use of "church" language is already an obstacle for some folks. Negative personal and historical experiences with "church" have a significant impact on our ability to have meaningful conversations about the "church." Too often, then, the baby is thrown out with the bathwater.

It is important, therefore, to establish a solid foundation for the intended nature of the "church" before we use the language too overtly. Thankfully, as already indicated above, it is not difficult to use other words to describe God's preference for historical peoplehood as the vehicle for the plan of global reconciliation.

Paul Minear, long-time scholar at Yale Divinity School,[5] uncovers 96 images used by New Testament writers to describe the nature, vocation, and function of the church. We already noted one of these images in the parable of the wheat and the weeds, i.e., "the children of the kingdom" (Mt. 13:38). There are 95 more. Some of these are familiar to us: body, temple, living stones; others are less so: ark, living letter, field. Even with these, there are 89 more. It is a rich menu designed to stimulate our imaginations. We must be careful not to create predetermined limits to any consideration of the expansive role and importance of the church envisioned in the New Testament.

---

[5] Paul Minear, *Images of the Church in the New Testament* (Westminster, 1960; re-issued in The New Testament Library, Westminster John Knox, 2004)

We don't need to discuss all of Minear's work here. It is available for those who so desire it. It is, however, a dramatic alert and reminder that we should not toy too lightly with notions of marginalizing the centrality of the church in our considerations of related themes, such as mission, discipleship, peace, and salvation. The mere existence of his investigation already leads us into serious questions and reflection. It is a reminder that we should not move too quickly. We need to take time to appreciate the images that he has uncovered.

Why does the New Testament cultivate such an extensive and creative focus on understanding the nature of an eschatological and historical peoplehood? This, surely, is not coincidence: it is woven into the fabric of the message from Matthew's Gospel to the book of Revelation.

Each image seems to address a particular niche that is important in capturing the essence of this kingdom peoplehood. "Body" is especially concerned with the coordinated, concerted, communal nature needed for the healthy function of this peoplehood. "Salt" and "light" focus more directly on the mission of this peoplehood, indicating how it functions in a patch of weeds. A "public letter" speaks to the needed integrity of its word and deed. The "bride of Christ" speaks to the need for covenant, holiness, and purity. The "ark" references the task of protection – a safe place – in a dangerous and difficult journey. The "temple" points to the integrity of worship for the new community. The "children of the kingdom" is a reminder that the community functions as a demonstration plot for the mysterious presence of the kingdom in the world. The "New Jerusalem" paints a picture of what is meant to be. "Ambassadors of reconciliation" emphasizes the centrality of peace-making as the vocation of the church. And then there are 85 more.

These images function as a consortium of symbols. None is designed to stand by itself. All together they begin to paint a picture of this multifaceted, unity-in-diversity that is needed to function as seeds and as sowers of seeds of God's reign in the world. It is an integrated system of signs, none more or less important than the other. Each symbol is indispensable for the vocation of the whole. Of course, this array of symbols, spread out before us like the tail of a proud peacock, need not be limited to 96. Once we get the hang of it, and as long as we don't undermine what is already there, more images can certainly be added. They do not need to be funnelled through a narrower bundle called "church." "Church" is simply one more within the 96, but one which has gained prominence as an abbreviation of the whole. It is important to remember that "church" is made up of 96 creative pictures and also does not stand alone or apart from any of them.

However, 2000 years of experience has taught us that such an impressive array of images has generated several temptations for the church. One temptation is to select a few favourites from the 96 and ignore the ones that didn't make our top 10 list. While we can point to legitimate, exegetical support for the chosen preferences, the choice of preferred options also allows us to criticize those who opted for a different top 10 list. We can call each other heretics, each one substantially supported by appropriate biblical texts. We have succeeded in limiting the expansive nature of what is intended. None of the images, by itself, is meant to be a summary of the whole. Rather, each one adds its contribution to expand the whole, not to narrow its focus.

Another temptation is to add images to the 96 that substantially contradict the integrity of the symbolic system. The 96 are an invitation to creativity so let's add our own, we say. This is, of course, true. The system of symbols is designed to encourage creativity of understanding. But it is not fair to suggest that therefore anything goes. It does not. When we dig deeply into the system of 96, we discover that there is amazing coherence in the symbols' distinct focuses. One of these focuses, for example, is that all 96 paint a picture of communal identity. They are not images of self-serving, individualized favouritism between God and me.

The images serve as a creative and diverse yet coherent effort to clarify the central plank of God's reconciliation strategy. They are scattered all over the New Testament literature. There is no effort, anywhere, to collect them together into one robust, compelling vision of what it means to be the people of God. The closest we get to a sustained argument is the Letter to the Ephesians. But even that does not do justice to the multicoloured rainbow of images suggested by the alliance of New Testament writers.

Given the depletion of ecclesiological conviction in contemporary understandings of faith and spirituality, we must wonder whether the brilliant communication strategy of the New Testament failed. The very creativity that was designed to awe and ignite our imaginations has, it seems, served to overwhelm our imaginative capacity, thus limiting and marginalizing these images. They are brought on stage only for rare, insignificant cameo roles in the larger drama of doctrinal preferences. They have supporting roles but are not the stars as they were meant to be.

A Closer Look at Ekklesia (Church)

We are now ready to take a closer look at "church" as envisioned by the biblical writers.

Perhaps we should begin with a simple question: When was the church born? I trust that by now the reader is aware that this is kind of a trick question. The most popular answer is that Pentecost is the birthday of the church. This is when the Holy Spirit was poured out on the ragtag band of "kingdom of God – according to Jesus – followers." They were "all together in one place" (Acts 2:1) in Jerusalem. With the sound of a mighty wind, the Spirit "filled the entire house… and they… began to speak in other languages, as the Spirit gave them ability" (Acts 2:2-4).

The linguistic dispersion of Babel in Genesis 11 here is a blessing. Although the crowd outside the house came from all parts of the known world, each one could hear "in [their] own native language" (Acts 2:8), and they heard the kingdom of God followers telling in their own language "about God's deeds of power" (Acts 2:11). The diversity of cultures is embraced as a strategic tool of peoplehood. The gathered crowd try to understand what is going on.

This is followed by a sermon by Peter. He assures the crowd that these folks are not drunk (Acts 2:15). What has happened is in line with the older traditions. His quotations from the prophet Joel (Acts 2:17-21) and from David's words in the Psalms (Acts 2:25-28) serve as points of connection with the past. What has happened is new, but not really. It is one more start to an ongoing process. This is a renovated peoplehood but not a new one. They must not consider what has happened as disconnected from previous initiatives of God.

Pentecost is, thus, not really the day of the birth of the church. It is, rather, another celebration of a birthday of peoplehood that can and should be traced back to other times. Yes, there are new things added: the identity of Jesus as the long-awaited Messiah and his death on the cross and resurrection by God are the most important. But the kingdom of God followers did not see this as contradicting Jewish hope, but as confirming it. The overall purpose and strategy of God is not new. The intention of a historical peoplehood guided by God and by God's Spirit, to be a permanent source of blessing and reconstruction in the world, is not new. Pentecost has not only wings but roots. Those roots are an important part of nurturing continuity.

We have already noted in the previous chapter that there is nonstop effort – at least 96 times – in the New Testament to help us picture the vocation of what later came to be known as "church." According to the Book of Acts, one of these names – or images – seemed to stick for a while. It is the image of "the Way" (cf. Acts 9:2; 22:4; 24:14). Luke (author of Acts) tells us that even the name "Christian" was not used from the beginning (Acts 11:26). It was in Antioch, a gentile city distant from Jerusalem, where this name first came into prominence. It seems that before the name "Christian" was used, the followers of Jesus were known as people of the Way.

This is an important detail. It was possible to talk about the Jesus followers without calling them "Christian." It was also possible to speak about them without referring to them as "church." It seems clear, though, that once the word "church" was used, it quickly gained significant traction. It appears not at all in Mark, Luke, or John, and only four times in Matthew. But once we leave the four Gospels behind, the word is dominant and is used 73 additional times (NRSV). Perhaps the most significant tell-tale sign is that Luke, the only author with material in both camps, uses the word "church" not at all in his Gospel but 17 times in the Book of Acts. While the word "church" came into prominence well before the four Gospels were written, it appears that the Gospel writers were dedicated to carefully preserving and integrally representing the vocabulary of the earlier history.

We need to take a closer look at the Greek word normally translated into English as "church." It is the word *ekklesia*.

Ekklesia is actually a compound word in Greek: *ek-klesia*. The word *ek* means "out of," as in *ex-odus*: the way out. The word *klesia (kleseos)* means "a calling" or "a vocation." The verb form – meaning "to call" – is *kaleo*. Literally, then, *ekklesia* means someone (or many) who are called out, or apart, from the rest. They are chosen for a particular calling or vocation.

The use of *ekklesia* in the New Testament has two important historical antecedents or roots.

First, in the Greek world, especially before the time of the New Testament when Greece was experimenting with a form of democracy, the word *ekklesia* was a political word. It referred to those citizens selected to participate in the councils for decision-making, especially the Council in Athens. It was an assembly of persons chosen from among the population to govern local affairs. During Roman occupation in Palestine, of course, such democratic notions were not much used. But the idea of a congregated group with a special calling continued to be embedded in the Greek language.

Second, the word *ekklesia* is used many times in the authorized Greek translation of the Old Testament. This Greek translation is called the Septuagint. The Hebrew Old Testament was translated into Greek sometime in the second and third centuries before Christ. This translation uses the Greek word *ekklesia* to translate the Hebrew Old Testament word *qahal*. In our English translations of the Old Testament, we miss this connection because the Septuagint *ekklesia* is variously translated into English as "congregation" (Psalm 22:22), "assembly" (Exodus 16:3; I Samuel 17:47; Psalm 149:1), "company of peoples" (Genesis 48:4), or "assembly of the congregation" (Numbers 14:5). The point is that the Septuagint translators used the word *ekklesia* to translate the Hebrew sense of people gathered for special purposes. The New Testament writers, in turn, chose this Septuagint use of *ekklesia* to describe their sense of the new peoplehood being brought together in Christ. This is the word translated into English as "church."

The Paul of Ephesians plays with this word, although it is largely lost in the English translation:

> *I therefore, the prisoner in the Lord, beg [para-kaleo] you to lead a life worthy of the calling [kleseos] to which you have been called [kaleo]...* (Eph. 4:1).

Literally, the church is being called to be the church in a worthy manner.

This raises the question: Why did the early disciples of Jesus gravitate toward the word *ekklesia* in order to name and describe the heart of their own self-understanding? Given the political overtones of the word, it would have been somewhat risky. And given that there were dozens (96) of other images used to describe the vocation of the discipled community, why choose this word? Why did this word stick?

I am not aware of any definitive answer to this question, but two things seem likely. First, the very fact that the word had a political ring to it encouraged the early Christians to use this word. They too thought of themselves as a political presence in the world, albeit an alternative politic. Indeed, Paul, in Philippians, exhorts the community there to let their manner of life be worthy of the gospel of Christ (Phil. 1:27). The phrase translated as "manner of life" is the Greek word "politics" (*politeuomai*). Let your politics be worthy of Jesus' politics, says Paul.

Second, it is also very likely that the New Testament writers liked the word *ekklesia* because – via the Septuagint, which was surely the version they used most – they understood their Jesus movement to be directly connected to the previous Old Testament efforts of peoplehood formation. This was more than a linguistic connection. God has been at work from the beginning to form a covenanted people of God to help bring about God's plan for reconciling the world to its intended purposes.

What is clear is that the word "church" did stick and became a primary word that was used to describe the Jesus movement. But it was always understood to be an abbreviation that included other key elements – at least 95 of them.

It should be noted that *ekklesia* needs to be defined. It identifies a "vocation" or a "calling," but it does not tell us what it is. It is like the word *evangelion*, which is also a compound word meaning "good news." *Evangelion* simply announces that there is "good news," but the word itself does not tell us what it is. It requires definition; it needs to be filled with meaning.

The New Testament writers do not hesitate to fill up the definition. As we have noted above, Jesus and the early disciples/writers used at least 96 images to fill the "calling" with specific content. In other words, *ekklesia* cannot stand alone. Indeed, it means very little if left on its own. Somehow, the "vocation" must be filled with tasks, vision, purpose, and meaning.

For those of us living in the 21st century, the risk of decentring the "church" in our theological understandings is to discard not the church but the 96 ways of understanding the nature and vocation of peoplehood. In essence, this redefines discipleship, ethics, mission, incarnation, and salvation. The baby is thrown out with the bathwater. We are left to our own devices. More often than not, such devices are determined by what the church has become rather than by what it was meant to be. Contemporary or historic realities replace eschatological vision and purpose. Reality supplants aspiration. Is it any wonder that we are easily discouraged?

I should say a word about the most frequent critique, namely the "institutionalization" of the church. This, in turn, refers to what the church has become. "Institutionalization" as a bad thing is often compared to "spirituality" as a good, modern substitute. The institutionalization of the church is also contrasted to Jesus: "I like Jesus, but I can't stand the church." Or, some make distinctions between the church as an institution and the church as a movement. It should be evident by now that such critique and comparisons are skin-deep only. Jesus himself would be incapable of imagining his God-project without its integral foundation of committed peoplehood.

What does it mean to institutionalize? It refers to the capacity to implement something that is desired. What is desired can, of course, be good or bad. But in either case, the hope that it can be accomplished serves as the foundation of institutionalized effort.

Each of the 96 images we discussed earlier is a way of saying that certain qualities, dear to the heart of God, need to be implemented. Salt is to function as salt; light as light; a body as a body; a temple as a temple. The hope is that good ideas will see the light of day. They will be acted upon, not once or twice but habitually. It is worthwhile for good things to happen again and again. Good "institutions" are designed to make sure good things can be repeated.

Jesus was an institutionalizer. When he washed his disciples' feet, he asked that this good thing should be repeatedly observed (John 13:12-20). When he broke bread and blessed the wine, he requested that this be done over and over again (Luke 22:19). He did not intend healing to be a one-off. He didn't want teaching about the kingdom to stop when he left. He wanted his disciples to continue to clothe the naked, visit the prisoners, feed the hungry, and more. Most of all, Jesus wanted his kingdom-community-building efforts to continue. He instructed his disciples to go into all the world, teach, baptize, and create communities of continuity. Indeed, this is what he died for.

Attempts to provide ongoing relevance and capacity to good things is not a bad thing, even when such efforts need budgets, programs, training, and accountability. He sent his disciples to teach obedience to "everything that I have commanded you" (Matthew 28:20). All of this is spiritual agenda. It is spirituality in action. But even Jesus' ministry needed a financial support structure. They worked with a budget. Luke tells us that at least part of the budget for his kingdom of God ministry was provided by "Joanna…Susanna, and many others, who provided for them out of their resources" (Luke 8:3). It appears as if Jesus accepted money from rich women – "the wife of Herod's steward Chuza…" (Luke 8:3) – for his expenses. These expenses must have been substantial to keep 12 men going over several years.

I am not suggesting that the church – as it is – is beyond critique. Not at all. I am well aware of the need to restore the church. But whatever adjustment is made, it will be done in a way that, hopefully, will shape the future differently. Adjustments will make good things happen better. Structures are needed. Even a light needs a "lamp-stand" (Matthew 5:15). Every spirituality requires flesh for its existence. There is no non-institutionalized church. Some may institutionalize a building as a meeting place. Others may institutionalize meeting in the shade of a tree. Some want pastors, others want only lay leadership. Some want committees to ensure continuity; others will institutionalize the spontaneous use of spiritual gifts. Regardless of which picture or group of pictures we choose as our preferred method of being church, we will organize in some way to ensure that it can happen – more than once.

The point is that when the early Christians chose *ekklesia* as their preferred way of speaking about the community living under the authority of God's reign, they chose an image that needed to be filled with details of the vocation they felt called to. They were certain, however, that the vocation was intimately connected to Jesus of Nazareth – what he taught, how he lived, that he was crucified and raised to life.

The early Christians were not skimpy in what they included in the vocation; indeed, they were so generous that for most of us the vocation overflows with unrealized potential. And so it has been from the beginning. The disciples struggled to understand the "good news" that Jesus was inviting them to. The Corinthian church struggled with competing leadership. Women and men in Galatia struggled with their respective roles in this new humanity. The group in Ephesus wondered about how marriage and children fit in. The group in Rome debated its role as an oppressed, persecuted minority in territory occupied by a brutal empire. The Jerusalem group tried to understand its own role in their beloved families, synagogues, and temple, as well as with the teachers that had shaped them thus far, especially as related to circumcision and Levitical law. The Johannine community struggled to define a new identity after its separation from the synagogue. The good news needed to speak to the struggles faced by each community, not only to the struggles of others.

Not only were the early communities shaped by "gospel" and "church," their existential struggles reshaped how they understood "gospel" and "church." They contributed to defining both based on the struggles they faced. These were expanding enterprises, elastic in nature, and they must remain so today.

The Church as a Branch Entwined with the Vine

The Gospel of John (the Fourth Gospel) has often been described as unique. It is not included as a "synoptic" Gospel because it is different. And it is true; there are significant differences. In the Gospel of John, Jesus talks a lot, and in long discourses. This is something we don't see much in Matthew, Mark, or Luke. The chronology of Jesus' ministry is different. For example, the episode of Jesus in the temple overturning tables and driving out the animals and money changers is one of the first things Jesus does in the Fourth Gospel (2:13-23). This event comes close to the end of his ministry in the synoptic Gospels. In the Fourth Gospel, Jesus is not baptized by John, as in the synoptics, but is immediately declared by John as "the Lamb of God who takes away the sin of the world" (1:29) and the "Son of God" (1:34). There is no messianic secret in the Fourth Gospel.

The Fourth Gospel has no birth narratives, no shepherds, star, wise men, or manger. It begins, rather, with a profound reflection about the coming of the "*logos*" (1:1-16). The *logos*, most often translated as "Word," is a reference to the wisdom and *torah* (law) of the Old Testament coming anew into the world. It goes unrecognized and even rejected by the world, with the exception of Jesus and the "children of God" (1:12) who receive the *logos* as a gift.

This shift in the way Jesus is presented has most often led scholars of the Fourth Gospel to focus on the nature of Jesus himself. In academic circles, this is referred to as "Christology." Given Jesus' very close relationship with God, who is most often referred to as the "Father" in this Gospel, discussion has focused on the high view of Jesus (i.e., high Christology). Some scholars have indeed said that in this Gospel Jesus is so divine that his feet barely touch the ground.

This focus on the nature of Jesus has, in turn, diminished the attention paid to the amazing vision of and for the church in the Fourth Gospel. It's true that Chapter 15 speaks of Jesus being the vine and his followers the branches, which is clearly an image of the importance of his community. But beyond that, considerations about the church (ecclesiology) have been overshadowed by attention to the nature of Jesus.[6] The fact that the word *ekklesia* or church is never used in the Fourth Gospel has helped to shift the focus away from the church, that is, Jesus' community of disciples.

In this chapter, we will take a closer look at a profound and amazing sense of "church" in this Gospel. It is so profound and so radical, in fact, that we will be tempted to disregard it outright.

There are two keys to detecting this Gospel's sense of church. One is to note carefully the authority attributed to Jesus. The other is the indelible solidarity that is constructed between Jesus and his discipled community. Authority and solidarity, we will discover, are shared and reciprocal attributes between Jesus and his followers. It is this shared, reciprocal relationship that is the foundation of the Fourth Gospel's sense of "church." This relationship is the focus of this chapter.

There is no one piece of definitive proof that secures the case for reciprocal authority between Jesus and his community. Rather, the Gospel develops an entire system of images that points us in a direction of understanding the profound solidarity. I will provide only a small sampling here of the way the solidarity is developed and, thus, the authority is shared.

---

[6] The first Nicene Creed (325 c.e.), for example, has a substantial section about the nature of Jesus and no word about the church. The second – and longer – Nicene Creed (381 c.e.) added a short statement about the church.

> *On that day you will know that I am in my Father, and you in me, and I in you. They who have my commandments and keep them are those who love me; and those who love me will be loved by my Father, and I will love them and reveal myself to them.... Those who love me will keep my word, and my Father will love them, and we will come to them and make our home with them (14:20-23).*

In this passage, mutual indwelling is shared among God, Jesus, and the community. The community becomes the new temple where God and Jesus can be "home" with each other and with the community.

> *I am the good shepherd. I know my own and my own know me, just as the Father knows me and I know the Father. And I lay down my life for the sheep (10:14-15).*

Knowledge of each other is reciprocal. Together we are known by God. There is a mutual relationship to the world, which includes the potential for persecution:

> *If the world hates you, be aware that it hated me before it hated you. If you belonged to the world, the world would love you as its own. Because you do not belong to the world, but I have chosen you out of the world – therefore the world hates you. Remember the word that I said to you, "Servants are not greater than their master." If they persecuted me, they will persecute you; if they kept my word, they will keep yours also (15:18-20).*

There is a mutual relationship with God:

> *All mine are yours, and yours are mine; and I have been glorified in them (17:10).*

> *I made your name known to them, and I will make it known, so that the love with which you have loved me may be in them, and I in them (17:26).*

> *On that day you will know that I am in my Father, and you in me, and I in you (14:20).*

There is reciprocal abiding and loving:

> *As the Father has loved me, so I have loved you; abide in my love. If you keep my commandments, you will abide in my love, just as I have kept my Father's commandments and abide in his love (15:9-10).*

The community is not only given the authority and the task of continuing the work of Jesus, but that "greater works than these" will be possible through the community of Christ.

> *Very truly, I tell you, the one who believes in me will also do the works that I do and, in fact, will do greater works than these, because I am going to the Father (14:12).*

Even the authority to judge and to forgive sin is passed on from Jesus to the disciples:

> *The Father judges no one but has given all judgment to the Son… (5:22).*

> *For just as the Father has life in himself, so he has granted the Son also to have life in himself; and he has given him authority to execute judgment, because he is the Son of man (5:26-27).*

> *Receive the Holy Spirit. If you forgive the sins of any, they are forgiven them; if you retain the sins of any, they are retained (20:22-23).*

Increasingly, the mission and authority of Jesus is indistinguishable from the mission and authority of the disciples.

Another technique used by the Fourth Gospel to build an unbreakable solidarity between Jesus and his followers is through the use of "from above" (*anothen*). It begins with the encounter between Jesus and Nicodemus (3:1-15). It is important to note the plural pronouns used: "Rabbi, **we** know…" (3:2). Nicodemus comes as a representative of "we." Who is that "we"? Given that he is introduced in 3:1 as a "Pharisee" and a "leader of the Jews," we must assume that the "we" is a reference to this group. Nicodemus is a spokesperson for himself and for others (cf. to plural responses by Jesus in 3:11). But note also Jesus' use of plural which includes himself: "…**we** speak of what **we** know and testify to what **we** have seen; yet you do not receive **our** testimony" (3:11).

The plural pronouns clearly indicate that this is a conversation between camps – between collective entities: the "leaders of the Jews" and the disciples of Jesus. Whether Jesus speaks for the disciples or the disciples speak for Jesus does not matter. Both are "born from above." Being "born from above" refers to the "Son of Man" (3:13-14), the "Son of God" (3:16-17), and to the faithful community (3:3-7).

This partnership that shares the divine characteristics of those "born from above" is already foreshadowed in the prologue. The Word (*logos*) unites with flesh (1:14), and the flesh is full of glory (*doxa*) (1:14). That same glory (*doxa*) is later given by Jesus to his community:

> *The glory that you have given me I have given them, so that they may be one, as we are one, I in them and you in me, that they may become completely one, so that the world may know that you have sent me and have loved them even as you have loved me* (17:22-23).

Both Jesus and the disciples are "flesh" (*sarx*) who bear the marks of the "glory" (*doxē*) of God. The solidarity is inseparable.

There are still other indicators of solidarity. There is the call to be servants and to wash feet (13:12-20), the hatred and rejection by the world (15:18-27), the sending and receiving of the Spirit (14:15-31; 20:22), and functioning as the sent ones of God (20:21).

Yet another passage takes the solidarity another step or two further. 10:31-33 intensifies the controversy between the Jewish establishment and Jesus as they take up stones to kill Jesus for blasphemy, saying, "It is not for a good work that we are going to stone you, but for blasphemy, because you, though only a human being, are making yourself God" (10:33).

The response of Jesus is intriguing indeed. He begins by quoting from Psalms 82:6: "I say, 'You are gods, children of the Most High, all of you.'" He then outlines in summary form what it means to be a *Son of God* (10:35-39): receive the word of God, do the works of the Father, be sanctified by the Father, and be sent into the world by the Father. We must note, however, that each of these traits is also attributed to the disciples:

- they have received the word (17:6-8);

- they have been sent into the world (17:18; 20:21);

- they have been sanctified for the work (17:19);

- they are doing the works of the Father (14:12-14).

The solidarity between the community of Jesus and Jesus himself continues to be built in every way possible. John 17 serves as a summary so far: the community has received and kept his Word (*logos*), the community and Jesus are both glorified, they experience divine unity, they are not of this world, they are rejected by the world, they are sanctified in truth, they are sent into the world, they are consecrated, and have the same destiny. The triangular solidarity is clear:

> ...that they may all be one. As you, Father, are in me and I am in you, may they also be in us, so that the world may believe that you have sent me (17:21).

Yet another example of solidarity is the treatment in the Gospel of the anonymous *disciple whom Jesus loved*. He is *reclining* next to Jesus

(13:23) as Jesus is *close to the heart of the Father* (1:18).[7] He shares with Jesus the knowledge of the identity of the betrayer (13:23-26). The Beloved Disciple is the true witness to Jesus (20:30; 21:25) and is the authority behind the Gospel (21:24-25). The Beloved Disciple functions as the Holy Spirit in the Johannine community. Just like the Holy Spirit that Jesus tells the disciples about, the Beloved Disciple remains with the disciples (14:17), teaches them (14:26), reminds them of what Jesus had said (14:26), declares what he heard (16:13), and glorifies Jesus because of what he receives and declares (16:14). This is not to say that the Beloved Disciple is the Holy Spirit. But the solidarity of function and presence between Jesus and the paradigmatic disciple – the authoritative teacher – is striking.

And then there is one further indication of solidarity that needs to be mentioned. The Fourth Gospel uses the *I am* formula about 20 times – each time as a reference to Jesus' solidarity with God. But there is one usage that is unique. It comes in Chapter 9. This chapter is likely a symbolic autobiography of the Johannine community. Like the blind man, this community was blind but now sees, while the Jewish leadership sees but is blind. After the blind man was healed, there was confusion about his identity:

> *Some were saying, "It is he." Others were saying, "No, but it is someone like him." He kept saying, "***I am*** *the man (9:9).*

If this were the only sign of solidarity in the Gospel, this occurrence could, perhaps, be explained as coincidence. There is nothing in the grammar that would suggest anything other than the normal use of *I am*. But we have seen how carefully and intentionally the pattern of solidarity is developed and how, in this chapter, the paradigmatic community of Jesus is developed. We see the care with which this Gospel uses this formula in the other uses. It would not be doing justice to the intention

---

[7] Both 1:18 and 13:23 use the Greek word *kolpos,* often translated as *bosom.* The NRSV chooses to translate this word variously as *reclining next to* and *close to the heart of.*

of this passage to see it as merely coincidental, or grammatically normal. It appears to be one more example of a carefully planned emphasis creating full solidarity between Jesus and his community.

What do we make of this developed pattern of solidarity and authority? I mentioned at the beginning of this chapter that nowhere is the word "church" used in the Fourth Gospel. But a new community is being created. This community, similar to what we will see in Ephesians, is to represent the *fullness of Christ* (Ephesians 1:22-23). This pattern helps us to understand the image of the vine and the branches (15:1-17), which is more overtly a reference to the community of disciples.

The pervasive pattern also allows us now to understand the prologue of the Gospel better. We can see that it is not simply a statement about Christ as has most often been suggested. It also speaks profoundly about the community that Jesus was creating – the children of God. The *Word (logos)*, which itself is a fusion of law and wisdom (*torah* and *khockma*), is eternally with God. It has come into the world in the manner of Jesus, and the world has not recognized it, nor him. But some children have recognized and accepted the Word:

> *But to all who received him, who believed in his name, he gave power to become children of God, who were born, not of blood or of the will of the flesh or of the will of man, but of God* (1:12-13).

The *children of God* are flesh born of and a home for the *logos* that has already been enfleshed in Jesus.

> *And the Word became flesh and lived among* [in; Greek *en*] *us, and we have seen his glory, the glory as of a father's only son, full of grace and truth* (1:14).

What we see here is, again, the same reciprocal solidarity that we have outlined above. Not only has the divine been enfleshed in humanity, humans are now agents of the divine. What is celebrated here is the full humanity of Jesus filled by the divine *logos*. This same potential characterizes the *children of God, born of God*. The Gospel, with its themes of solidarity and authority, works hard to narrow the divinity gap between Jesus and his community. The calling for the community of disciples could not be higher. The identification of Jesus with this community could not be more integral.

The key to the ongoing solidarity and authority of the Johannine community as paradigmatic of the presence of Jesus himself is the presence of the Holy Spirit in the community. Only in the Fourth Gospel does the community of Jesus receive the Holy Spirit via the *breathing* of Jesus himself:

> *When he had said this, he breathed on them and said to them, "Receive the Holy Spirit"* (20:22).

The breathing of the life of the Spirit is surely reminiscent of the creation of humanity by God:

> *…then the Lord God formed man from the dust of the ground, and breathed into his nostrils the breath of life; and the man became a living being* (Gen. 2:7).

Jesus, in the Fourth Gospel, is re-creating humanity. The new community now functions as the Spirit because the Spirit is with them, in them, and among them. Just as Jesus received the Spirit (1:32-33) the community has now undergone the baptism of the Spirit from the breath of Jesus himself. This authorizes the community to forgive and retain sins (20:23). In a sense, the community has now also become the *Lamb that takes away the sins of the world* (1:29). The authority of Jesus has been shared with the community.

The creation of the new community of Jesus in the Fourth Gospel is truly breathtaking. Yet, it is not significantly different from what we see in the synoptic Gospels, in Ephesians, or in other parts of the New Testament writings. But it seems to be more scandalous and more brazen. The community is the presence of divinity itself. For us moderns, this is hard to swallow and difficult to stomach. This was also true of the Jewish community of the first century. This Gospel is relentless in its high calling of the community of disciples (the church). In the Fourth Gospel at least, the plan of God for the redemption of the world is constructed around the presence of the community of the Spirit, authorized to function as the ongoing presence of Jesus in the world.

Scandalous, yes. Indeed, the Fourth Gospel presents us with two significant scandals. One is that God can be enfleshed in human community. The other is that human community can be authorized to function under divine authority and with divine solidarity. Such is the vision that is before us. We discard parts of such a high calling at the peril of losing it all. Again, the image of throwing out the baby with the bathwater is pertinent for us.

Robert Kysar, an eminent Johannine scholar, has helpfully articulated what any serious reading of the Fourth Gospel puts on our plate. The categories we have at our disposal to understand what is going on are not adequate to understand what we find in this Gospel.

Kysar says:

> ... [There is] a crying need for new categories by which to comprehend the ideas of the evangelist and in particular the relationships among some of the major motifs of his Gospel. The categories recently employed are burdened with modern connotations which get in the way of their elucidation of the evangelist; or they are so narrow as to be inadequate... It is my contention that the evangelist's own basic categories have not yet been discovered.[8]

I will mention only two often-used categories that seem to "get in the way," and which are blown apart by a close reading of this Gospel.

---

[8] Robert Kysar, *The Fourth Evangelist and his Gospel* (Minneapolis: Augsburg Publishing House, 1975), p. 279

One is the sharp distinction we make between divinity and humanity. The Fourth Gospel tramples all over such categorical distinctions. Yes, the Gospel's portrait of Jesus is very elevated, but then so is its portrait of the human community. If we feel uncomfortable with such a high view of humanity, then we keep the "humanity" category lower; but then the portrait of Jesus must follow suit, and we feel uncomfortable with what that would mean for our understanding of Jesus. The shared solidarity and authority between Jesus and his community simply doesn't seem to fit our definitions of divinity and humanity, neither in the ways it applies to Jesus nor in how it applies to his community of disciples.

A second category that does not seem to fit is a doctrinal understanding of Trinity that somehow stands apart from the creation of the community which has inherited the authority and ministry of Christ himself. The profound solidarity and shared authority among God, Son, Holy Spirit, and the community, which we have sketched above, does not adequately fit into our created category of "Trinity." In simple mathematics, it adds up to more than three.

In some sense, then, the Fourth Gospel's insistence on reciprocal solidarity and mutual authority between Jesus and his community causes a problem for us. We have created categories that don't seem to fit the text. Indeed, it is almost as though our categories make the text itself heretical. The text gets in the way of our doctrinal preferences. Kysar suggests that it's the other way around. Actually, he says, our categories get in the way of understanding the text. We can't fully embrace the text because of the pre-established categories we use as a lens to read it.

If we can modify our embedded lenses, we will note that what the Fourth Gospel sketches is not substantially distinct from the image of wheat among weeds, of communities of the kingdom of God in hostile territory as articulated in the synoptic Gospels. We will also note that what the Fourth Gospel sketches is not substantially distinct from the church as an expression of the *fullness of him* in the midst of principalities and powers as suggested in Ephesians. One of the modifications we will need to make is to recover the profound sense of "church" in the Fourth Gospel. It is a Gospel deeply concerned about understanding our vocation as communities of disciples of Jesus. It focuses at least as much on the question of what it means to be the church as it does on defining the nature of Jesus. If we miss that profound link, the baby disappears with the bathwater.

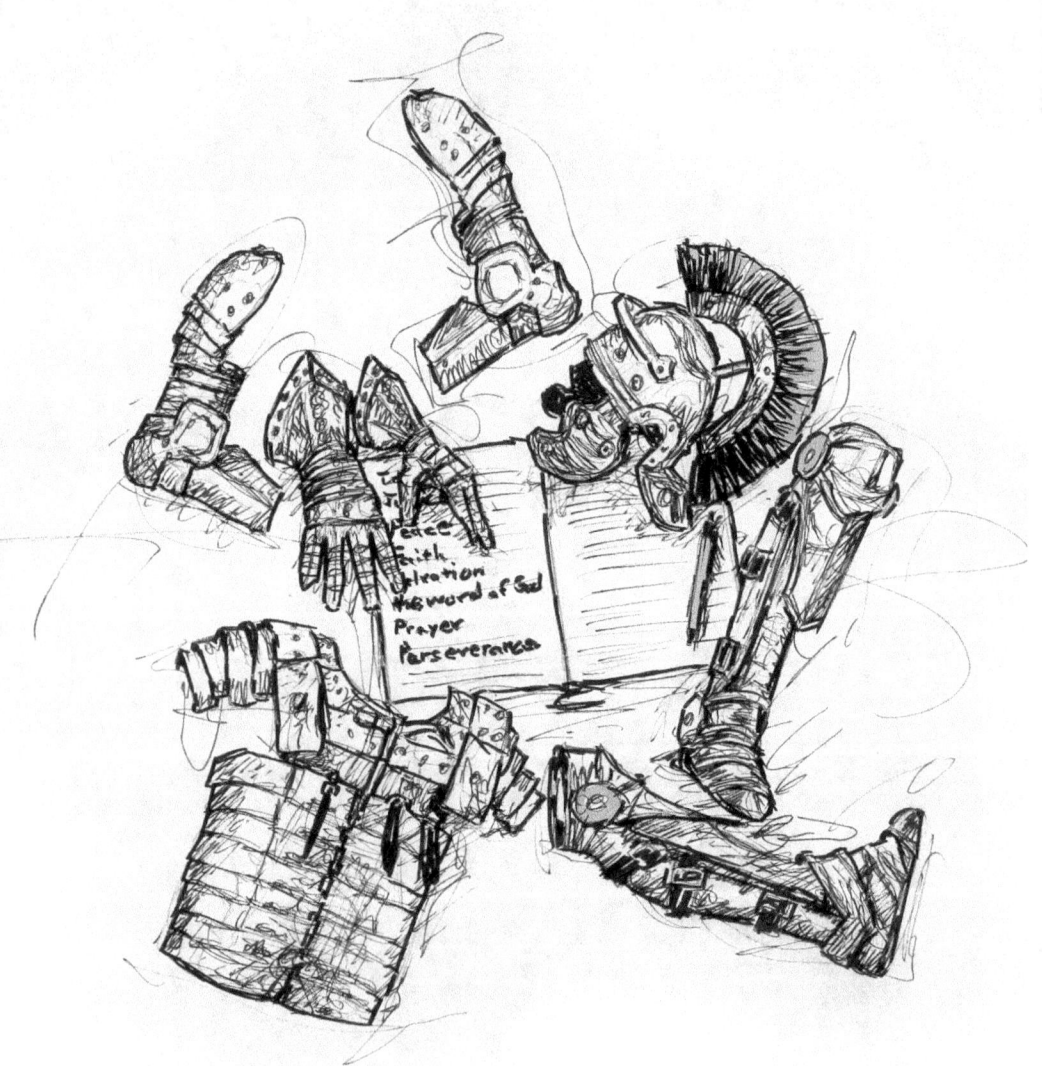

The Church as Teacher

The Letter to the Ephesians lays out another breathtaking vision of the nature, purpose, and vocation of the church. It is the most comprehensive and intricate argument available to us from the New Testament writers. It is worth our while to take a closer look.

Chapter 1 is a gush of effusive praise and gratitude for what God has done. God has *blessed us in Christ with every spiritual blessing* (1:3); *chosen us* (1:4); *destined us* (1:5); and has *freely bestowed glorious grace* (1:6). God has *lavished on us the riches of his grace* (1:7-8); we have *redemption and forgiveness* (1:7); we can *live for the praise of his glory* (1:12); we have *heard the word of truth and salvation* (1:13); and *believed in him* (1:13). We have been called to *hope … of the riches of his glorious inheritance* (1:18); and *the immeasurable greatness of his power* (1:19). This opening summary leaves us breathless with expectation for what is to come. The exuberant spirit of gratitude, potential, and hope makes us sit back and take a deep breath to help us digest this torrent of praise. The grammar itself gives us a clue to the urgency and hope of the message: 1:3-14 – in the Greek text – is all one sentence. It is as if a marathon runner has run from Sparta to Athens to announce victory in the battle – out of breath, very excited.

There are, however, also serious reminders of our responsibilities in the midst of all this blessing. God *has made known to us the mystery of his will* (1:9); and has provided a *spirit of wisdom and revelation in our knowledge of him* (1:17). Our *hearts have been enlightened so that we may know the hope to which we have been called (klesis)* (1:18). We can't simply sit back, relax, and gush. We are called to serious participation in this process. There is a vocation at stake here. We are privileged to be part of this calling. But it will require serious effort on our part to understand what is expected.

The chapter does not leave us in the dark about what this vocation is. The *mystery* has been revealed (1:9). We now know for sure what God wants and what God is calling us to: *as a plan for the fullness of time, to gather up all things in him, things in heaven and things on earth* (1:10). God is in the business of *gathering up* all things, all things, all things (in case we didn't get it the first or second time). God is in the process of bringing together both heaven and earth under one authority. This is the dream of God. We will notice, as we continue to read the letter, that this mission of God is handed over for implementation to the church. God's mission defines the purpose and the vocation of the church.

The Greek word translated as *gather up* is *anakefaleo*. *Ana* means "again," and *kefaleo* means "to be the head of," or "have authority over." It is very similar to the well-known concept of "kingdom of God." It points to an effort to re-establish the authority of God as the operating principle in creation. It brings everything together, reconciles all to its original purposes. This word is used only one other time in the New Testament, in Romans 13:9 (translated as *summing up*). Here, Paul is summarizing the basics of the original intentions of God (Romans 13:8-14): love one another, love the neighbour, *put on [enduo] the Lord Jesus Christ* – as if Jesus were a coat we can wear.

This sense of "wearing Jesus" (or God) is further defined in Ephesians 6:11-18 where the church is urged to *put on* the whole armour of God: truth, justice, peace, faith, salvation, the word of God, prayer, and perseverance. It is further amplified in Colossians 3:12-17 where *putting on* God's intentions include: compassion, kindness, lowliness, meekness, patience, forbearing, forgiveness, love, peace, teaching one another in wisdom, singing psalms, and gratitude. These are some of the tools in the toolkit, useful to the saints in *gathering up all things* so that they can be as they were always intended.

What is clear is that God's plan for reconciliation is more than big; it is cosmic. There is nothing, nothing, nothing that is not included. The modern lament we hear too often is that connecting with the "church" is too limiting; the agenda is too narrow. We want to engage the world, have interfaith partnerships and dialogue, initiate social change, heal the politics of our nation, care for the environment, and end oppressive systems. The church's agenda is too narrow, too limited, too restrictive. Some insist that we need to disengage from the church to free us to do the work of God.

This sentiment is entirely contradictory to the vision of God for the church as articulated in Ephesians. Every other plan we can imagine sounds anemic to this one. There is no other plan as comprehensive as this one – they are all niche plans. And the church is called to be an agent of this cosmic plan of God. The mystery of purpose is now known. The power that was at work in the resurrection is now available to the church (1:19-20). Its reach includes *all rule and authority and power and dominion, and every name that is named, not only in this age but also in that which is to come* (1:21). The agenda doesn't get bigger than this. It is epic; it is all-encompassing.

God has *put all things under the feet* (1:22) of the Lordship of Jesus, who is the *head (kefale) – for the church* (1:22). In other words, there is a chain of authority here: God to Jesus and Jesus to the church. And the church? It is *his body, the fullness of him who fills all in all* (1:23). Talk about breathtaking; the description of the "church" as the *fullness of him* is awe-inspiringly astounding. It overwhelms our sensitivities. We're tempted to think that it is surely too high a view of us, or of the church, and that our job undeniably must be to lower expectations – that this is just too much. In this chain, the church is the agent of the authority of Christ who, in turn, is exercising the authority of God over all things.

But this is indeed the vocation (calling) of the church. It is not a narrow, limited, restricted agenda. There is nothing that is not the agenda of the church.

The rest of the Letter to the Ephesians provides further insight and detail about this rather incredible calling of the church. We will not go into the same level of detail, but once we allow the challenge of Chapter 1 to sink in, we will see how the rest of the letter underlines how this is all supposed to function.

Chapter 2 uses several images to speak of the nature of the church. It is the *household of God* (2:19) built on the *foundation of apostles and prophets* (2:20). Jesus is the *cornerstone* (2:20), and as such the *structure is joined together and grows into a holy temple .... a dwelling place of God* (2:21-22).

Household of God, holy temple, a dwelling place of God – surely a stunning honour and responsibility. But the key to the chapter is the description of who makes up this household, temple, and dwelling place. There used to be a wall of separation dividing the Jews and the Gentiles (2:11-13). But under the plan of God to unite all things, those barriers have been removed. Reconciliation has come, thus creating *one new humanity* (2:14-15). Christ *is our peace* (2:14). Former enemies or life-contenders are now in *one body* (2:16), hostilities have ended, and peace has come (2:16-17). Strangers and sojourners are now *citizens with the saints* (2:19). Notice the generous helping of images used in this short passage to describe the church. The world is no longer the same. The reunification plan of God is already functioning, with the key mechanism being the cross of Christ that enables community. It is a costly process of reconciliation. Indeed, it is sacrificial. But it is on the way. And the renewed existence and vocation of the church is the first fruits of this process.

Chapter 3 continues unabated, pushing the vocation a few more steps. Again, Paul begins with reference to the *mystery* (3:3-4) and how he has been tapped on the shoulder as a special agent of the mystery due to the *commission of God's grace* (3:2). It is a new insight *not known to humankind in other generations* (3:5). And the revealed insight is: *how the Gentiles have become fellow heirs, members of the same body, and sharers in the promise in Christ Jesus through the gospel* (3:6). While this is not different from the creation of the *new humanity* in Chapter 2, it is so remarkable that it is worth repeating.

But the punchline is still to come, with another remarkable insight:

> ***...so that through the church*** *the wisdom of God in its rich variety might now be made known to the rulers and authorities in the heavenly places. This was in accordance with the eternal purpose that he has carried out in Christ Jesus our Lord* (3:10-11).

Surely these five words are some of the most important words in the New Testament: ***so that through the church...*** If this does not give us goosebumps, we are numbed, apathetic zombies. This affirmation demands serious reflection. The church's vocation is to function as a teacher – a pedagogue – to the *principalities and powers* so that they too may be reconciled to the intentions for which they were created.

We have already been introduced to the controlling *rule and authority and power and dominion and name* (1:21) that have been *put under the feet* of Jesus and the church (1:21-23). Here in Chapter 3, the church is given an additional task with the *principalities and powers* (3:10), and it is a pedagogical task. The church is to *make known* (3:10) the revealed mystery to powers. The church is not only a carrier of information, it is the teacher of what it knows. Again, we must stand back in amazement and let this sink in. What a staggering vocation assigned to the church. The chapter ends with another invocation of worship, benediction, and gratitude for the love and knowledge, so that we *may be filled with all the fullness of God* (3:19): a reminder of what we already heard in 1:22-23.

The vocation of the church has been clarified, and it is truly remarkable; indeed, it is breathtaking. Chapter 4 then begins with a petition to "lead a life worthy of the calling to which you have been called…" (4:1). This is an artful play on words. *Calling* and *called* are both built on the same root word as *ek-klesia* (cf. chapter on *ekklesia*). Just as God's purpose is to *gather up all things* (1:10), the church is the demonstration plot of unity. There is "one body and one Spirit … one hope of your calling, one Lord, one faith, one baptism, one God and Father of all…" (4:4-6).

So, specifically, how can the church fulfill the mandate it has been assigned? Chapter 4 goes on to explain how this amazing vocation can be put into practice. It centres around the exercise of the spiritual gifts that the ascended Christ has given to each one. The *body of Christ* (4:12) has been given the *equipment (katartismos)* to function well (4:12). This is the only place in the New Testament where this Greek word is used as a noun, not as a verb. The *apostles, prophets, evangelists, pastors and teachers* (4:11) are the equipment of the saints. With these gifts the entire community can function as a body, united in *faith and the knowledge of the Son of God* (4:13), with *maturity* and *to the measure of the full stature of Christ* (4:13). Notice how this sense of *fullness* is again repeated. The church has what it needs to do what it is designed to do. I am reminded of an elderly lady who, with a warm smile and glowing eyes, said to me, "Our congregation is like a little songbird. We have everything we need to be who we are." The chapter closes with a lengthy litany of how life under the authority of God must be lived.

Chapter 5:1-6:9 digs in even deeper. Here, Paul provides three additional windows into life when it is lived under the new reality of the now-revealed vocation of the church. We have already seen what happens to the relationships between Jews and Gentiles. Now he identifies three more common realities: how does this impact marriage and the relationship between husband and wife; how does this impact the relationship between parents and children; and how does it impact the relationship between master and slave? In each case, the existing cultural and political assumptions are inverted.

Subjection between husband and wife is a mutual obligation (5:21). The *honour* of parents must be accompanied by fathers who *do not provoke children to anger* (6:2-4). And masters must treat slaves with *no partiality* (6:9) and with the same respect that slaves must treat masters: it is a mutually nurturing relationship (6:6-9). Paul is creating a new social/economic system built on the foundation of a new social order.

Slavery, for example, cannot survive under the conditions mandated here. That system will crumble. Neither can patriarchy survive. It too will disintegrate. Truly *all things* are being reconciled by God, and the church is the demonstration plot for how this will work.

The crescendo of the vision for the church is saved for the last section: 6:10-23. Here, the armour that was used by God to intervene in the systemic injustice that was evident everywhere (Isaiah 59:1-17) is given to the church. In Isaiah there was *no justice,* and *there was no one to intervene* (Isaiah 59:15-16). God was *displeased* (Isaiah 59:15) by this situation and put on the armour necessary to step in. In Ephesians, this is changed. Paul instructs the church to *put on the whole armour of God* (6:11):

> *For our struggle is not against enemies of blood and flesh, but against the rulers, against the authorities, against the cosmic powers of this present darkness, against the spiritual forces of evil in the heavenly places. Therefore take up the whole armor of God, so that you may be able to withstand on that evil day, and having done everything, to stand firm* (6:12-13).

We have seen, by now, an impressive array of evil and powers lined up against the coming authority of God on earth. These include principalities, powers, spiritual armies of evil, world rulers, rule, authority, power, dominion, and names. These are *not flesh and blood* but are the dominant reality behind what makes us do what we do. They could be embedded in culture, educational assumptions, economic systems, social norms, political processes, philosophies, family systems, institutional organization, religions, ethics, and much more. No wonder the task of *gathering up all things* is a giant task. It is easy to be overwhelmed by this system of resistance to God's authority taking root. Yet, the task of the church is to *stand* (6:13-14) and *stand firm* (6:13), to teach the powers the mystery of God's plan (3:10) and invite their cooperation in it. Notice there is no sense here of destruction or annihilation of the powers. There is only a sense of reconciling them to function within the limits that God sets for them. They too are under higher authority. They are not independent monsters with no higher accountability (cf. also Colossians 1:16).

The instruments of the armour are identified. The church is equipped with eight pieces: truth, justice, the gospel of peace, faith, salvation, the word of God, prayer, and perseverance. We note, however, that *vengeance and fury* (Isaiah 59:17) are left out. These are not suitable as armour for the church. Corruption cannot withstand truth; violence cannot withstand peace; inequality cannot survive the presence of justice. When the church is the church, the powers begin to tremble. The alliance of truth with justice, perseverance with prayer, salvation with faith, and peace with God's word is strength and power. It is the power of resurrection life at work creating life in abundance. It is the power of the church at work.

A Community of Hope

This final chapter is important because it makes more explicit what has been implicit throughout the book thus far. It is especially important for those who are discouraged because of the very significant gap between the aspiration for the church in the biblical text and the reality of what the church is and has been. How do we live and function helpfully within this evident incongruity?

The church is a community of hope.

Community and communion share the same root word in English. This is true also in the Greek of the New Testament. The Greek word is *koinonia*. This is a remarkably versatile word and carries meanings of sharing, partnership, giving, receiving, solidarity, and participation with each other. It is also the word that grounds our understanding of the Lord's Supper or Eucharist:

> *The cup of blessing that we bless, is it not a **sharing** in the blood of Christ? The bread that we break, is it not a **sharing** in the body of Christ?* (I Cor. 10:16).

The church of Christ has *koinonia* in Christ as its foundation. In a profound exploration of *koinonia* in the New Testament, one scholar states:

> *It is clear that koinōnia is an identity-giving, life-shaping, commitment-forging, and action-provoking gift of God.*

> *We receive it with Christ standing among us and his*
> *Spirit enabling us to both receive and exercise this gift.*[9]

To speak of the church as a "community" or as a "communion" is, then, no small thing. *Koinonia* penetrates the meaning and purpose of "church" as salt penetrates the Dead Sea.

The Greek noun for hope – *elpis* – is used 53 times in the New Testament. Hope is more than optimism. Optimism still assumes that if only we do the right things, then things will get better. Our friends in Colombia used to say that: "Hope is possible only when we can no longer be optimistic. We have decided to postpone our pessimism until times get better."

They are on to something important. Hope is more than simple strategic expectation. It is expectation based on deep trust and confidence in something – or someone – beyond our capacity to know fully or to plan precisely. It is the expectation of something that is certain and assured but not yet fully visible or complete. The Apostle Paul says it well:

> *For we know only in part, and we prophesy only in part; but when the complete comes, the partial will come to an end* (1 Cor. 13:9-10).

The Letter to the Hebrews says:

> *Now faith is the assurance of things hoped for, the conviction of things not seen* (Heb. 11:1).

How can we describe the spiritual makeup of a community (*koinonia*) that lives with assurance – but on the basis of partial knowledge? Or one that functions on a foundation of things not seen? Clearly, it is a slippery task to try to identify the essential fabric of such a community. But we will try to describe this – at least to some degree.

---

[9] Thomas R. Yoder Neufeld, "Koinonia: The Gift We Hold Together" (Mennonite Quarterly Review, July, 2012), p. 348

The biblical vision for the church as a community of hope presupposes at least four spiritual attributes that must form the backbone of such a community.

The first attribute is that the church is a doxological community. Doxology is a Greek compound word: *doxē*, meaning glory, and *logos* meaning word. A doxological community, then, is one that puts God and the glory of God at its centre and proclaims it as foundational for its own existence. The Fourth Gospel describes this best:

> *The glory that you have given me I have given them, so that they may be one, as we are one* (Jn. 17:22).

The glory that was seen in the Son (Jn.1:14) now also forms part of the nature of the community. What does it mean to be a community of glory? Perhaps the most important thing is that it helps us to recognize that the community itself is not the final word: God is. The mission is not ours; it is God's. The community does not live for itself only, nor does it live on its resources alone. Glory is a God-quality, and a community that understands itself as a community of glory acknowledges only partial knowledge and hopes in things as yet unseen.

This attribute is most often expressed in worship and prayer. Both are ways of saying that we worship a God who knows more than we do and who sees things that are still not visible to us. Doxology generates humility because it reminds us that there is only one God, and it is not us. Doxology allows us to both stand firm and to let go. We walk with assurance and, at the same time, we relinquish ultimate control to God. Doxology helps us to not lose courage and to live in the paradox between aspiration and reality. Worship and prayer are humble expressions of gratitude as we acknowledge that God is God, and we are not.

A second attribute of a community of hope is its eschatological nature. Eschatology too is a Greek compound word: *eschatos*, meaning the last of something old that makes room for something new to begin, and *logos*, meaning word. A community of *eschatos*, then, is one that proclaims the possibility of a new future – the start of something better.

Note that eschaton does not mean "end" in the sense of moving from something to nothing. While it is the last of a series of things, it is followed by something else: a new start.

It is not an exaggeration to say that the entire Bible is eschatological. It rests on a vision that what is now will be transformed into something different and better. This "something" too is out of the hands of human endeavour alone. Again, God is an actor; the eschaton and what follows is in God's hands. But it is assured, and therefore it too is an attribute of hope. The church is an agent of the eschaton, keeping alive a vision of something that is yet to come. Our reality, which does not yet match with what will be, is not meant to discourage us. It is designed to strengthen our dependence on the glory of God, on hope lived in faith, and on confidence in what is yet to be. The vision for the church as sketched in the previous chapters is energized by eschatological hope. Eschatology too demands humility on the part of the church. While we are important actors, we are not the director of what is being played out among and before us.

A third attribute of a community of hope is that it functions as a sacrament in a world in great need of reconciliation and salvation. Sacrament is a Latin word referring to an oath or a pledge. It is a sign or a promise of something yet to come. The Catholic Church suggests that the church is the "universal sacrament of salvation."[10] I believe it is helpful to think of the nature of the church as a pledge (promise) or a sign of salvation. This assigns eternal purpose to the church and not only to God. The idea is that when folks see, experience, or get in contact with the church, they should sense in it the promise of something better – for themselves and for the world. We have shown in the preceding chapters that the church is designed to be an agent of God for the salvation of the world. As such, it is a sacramental presence, a promise of what is yet to come. The church is already in part what it is meant to become more fully.

---

[10] Lumen Gentium (Light of the Nations): This is a document of the Second Vatican Council, focusing on the church as the "People of God."

The fourth attribute of a community of hope is that it is to be the visible presence within humanity of God's loving purposes for the world. We call this "incarnation." Incarnation too has a Latin root; it means "in flesh." The church has the awesome vocation of enacting "in flesh" the glory that is in God. Flesh is something we can touch, feel, and see. It is not abstract. It is real. Incarnation is solidarity. It is God with us through thick and thin. And it is the community of God being with the world through thick and thin.

John's Gospel talks about the *Word* living *among us* (Jn. 1:14). The *torah* and the wisdom of God become palpable in Jesus and in a community of disciples. The proclamation of God's intentions is not words only. Proclamation is life visibly accessible in a community that lives under the authority of God.

Each of these spiritual attributes is wrapped up tightly in resurrection. The resurrection of Jesus, following closely upon the cruelty of the cross, is the ongoing assurance and power of God at work in the world. Death is not the final word. God's will is that there be life – life in abundance. The reign of death will be overcome with life.

The Letter of I Peter talks about the likelihood that the church will experience persecution and suffering. It will suffer because the powers that be will not understand it. Or if they do understand, they will not agree with what it stands for. Peter exhorts the church to be ready to defend the possibility of hope:

> *Always be ready to make your defense to anyone who demands from you an accounting for the hope that is in you; yet do it with gentleness and reverence. Keep your conscience clear, so that, when you are maligned, those who abuse you for your good conduct in Christ may be put to shame. For it is better to suffer for doing good, if suffering should be God's will, than to suffer for doing evil* (1 Pet. 3:15-17).

When things are not going our way, how is it that hope is still possible? How do we explain hope in times of persecution? How do we defend the possibility of hope in dark days? It is the task of the church to be prepared to do this – *always be ready.*

In summary, the essential nature of the church is doxological, eschatological, sacramental, and incarnational. Each of these is an expression of the reality of resurrection: the victory of life over the forces of death, now and into the future. They also express the conviction of solidarity and partnership *(koinonia)* within the diversity of the church, and with God. In the words of Dietrich Bonhoeffer, the church "is the presence of Christ in the same way that Christ is the presence of God."[11] As such, the church is a community of hope in a broken world.

May it be so.

---

[11] Dietrich Bonhoeffer quoted by Stanley Hauerwas in ABC Religion and Ethics, July 14, 2017: "Why Bonhoeffer matters: The Challenge for Christian ministry at the end of Christendom"

Appendix

Self-Audit: Taking Stock

We return now to the 21st century to take stock of what we have seen. In my case, I am reading the biblical text from a Canadian/North American context. My comments are undoubtedly influenced by my setting. But I do hasten to add that my analysis of the fate of the church is not North America-restricted. I have had the good fortune and incredible blessing of sitting with pastors and church leaders in at least 30 countries in the world. We have engaged deeply together, both about the struggles their churches face and about themselves as leaders. Above all, we have examined the biblical text and the inspirational view of the church we have sketched above.

In Canada, I have visited every one of the congregations of our denomination in their primary place of worship, and I have listened to them express their joys and pains as they too struggle to be the church in their home setting. I have had some level of oversight for the dozens of organizations and institutions birthed by the church to foster particular niches of ministry on behalf of the church. My experience with the church has not been limited to any particular denomination. I have been blessed by participation in broad circles of Christian ecumenical engagement and interfaith dialogue. My family and I have also lived and worked in four countries outside of Canada and have spent many years dedicated to the work of the church in these settings.

To speak of an "audit," then, is an exaggeration. The best I can hope for is to stimulate a series of "self-audits" in every nook and cranny in which

God has placed the church. Perhaps what we need is "self-examination" à la St. Ignatius, but applied not only to our personal, daily lives but organizationally to the lives of our churches and programs. I will share some reflections and experiences. I will name no names and throw no stones. I simply hope to reflect on what I have experienced, seen, and heard with the hope that this might stimulate others to do likewise.

To begin, I would encourage every congregation, denomination, and church-related organization to take a close look at the mission, vision, and purpose statements that guide your day-to-day ministry. Is there any sense of the urgency for being the church that we have noted in the biblical text? This exercise may not be as simple as it sounds. The guiding statements may well have some mention of the church, but that is not the question here. Do the statements express some sense of commitment to the cosmic nature and vocation of the church that we have noted? Do they see the church as both a demonstration and a vehicle of God's reconciliation plan? Do they express the urgency that the church be a high priority? Do they impact the strategy of ministry? How?

I have done a substantial amount of research into the exercise I have suggested above, including, but not only, organizations of my own denomination. The results are not encouraging. Indeed, it is evident that an overt, robust, and profound sense of the church's vocation has largely vanished from our vision. Congregations continue to articulate some sense of ecclesiology, but in a very limited and local sense and largely devoid of the cosmic importance of the church's vocation articulated in the biblical record.[12]

This exercise will reveal, I think, a series of temptations to which the church in its diversity has fallen prey. The 96 images that attempt to expand the purpose and vocation for the church (cf. Chapter 4) have been discarded in favour of a select few preferred by each church. It is not that the selected images are bad. But they have been restrictive,

---

[12] Some results can be found in Suderman, Robert (edited by Andrew G. Suderman). *Re-Imagining the Church*. (Wipf and Stock, Eugene, Oregon, 2016; cf. chapter 3, especially pps. 23-30).

and such limitations erode the urgent and cosmic purpose, nature and witness of the church.

In some churches, the strong sense of the church's vocation has been diverted into sacramental functions. As long as these churches continue to faithfully observe a limited number of functions or rituals that serve as salvific vehicles, they feel that they are fulfilling their foundational vocation as church. Other churches focus the ecclesial function on "spreading the Word." Taking the parable of the sower and the seed as a basis, they spread the Word among thistles and on arid and rocky ground. They believe that God will do the rest and will assure that the good soil is also nurtured with the Word. This is, of course, important, but is limiting the churchly vocation to 1 out of 96 of the New Testament list of images.

Some have understood the church's function as chaplaincy. This focus too is important, as it pays special attention to addressing the symptoms generated by the varieties of evil that confront our living. It heals the wounds, but stays away from prophetic functions of living and articulating an alternative to the roots and causes of the symptoms themselves. Still others see the role of the church as a handmaiden of the state. The state, they say, has the responsibility to create the acceptable framework for social interaction, and the church helps in making such interaction possible.

Other organizations and church bodies focus on discipleship to Jesus as their primary vocation. Too often, however, following Jesus does not inherently include a profound connection to discipleship in the communities of the kingdom that Jesus so evidently was committed to. Discipleship is more often than not understood as conversion and personal following without necessarily understanding ecclesial participation and accountability as part of the testimony. Others focus on "evangelism" and "conversion" as the primary niche of ministry. More often than not, however, their "good news" does not include a significant sense of the church's purpose, and "conversion" is personal and internal, thus lacking Jesus' intentions of the communal nature of conversion to the emerging kingdom among us. Potentially helpful living rituals, such as baptism and communion, have been downgraded to symbols of personal commitment to Jesus or rituals that aid the function of salvation.

Some understand their Christian niche ministry as activating "peace" that is so evident in the biblical witness. They have become specialists in understanding obstacles to peace, the dynamics of mediation, techniques of conflict transformation, and the need for community solidarity and development. But their textbooks and curricula are devoid of any sense of profound ecclesiology as a vehicle for the reconciliation of social or cosmic ills. Even our sense of salvation more often than not understands the role of the church as something subsequent to "salvation" and not integral to it.

Yet others focus more intensively on the presence of the Holy Spirit in our lives. They celebrate the gifts of the Spirit, speak in tongues, heal the sick, and drive out demons, but they forget that all of these too were signals of the kingdom emerging: a kingdom in which the Spirit is received in community and discerned in community, and where the discernment is implemented as communal expressions of kingdom living.

Some churches and organizations focus on institutional programming, doctrinal alignment, and social development. Each of these can function quite nicely without any significant or sustained attention to the church as the motor of God's intended reconciliation of creation.

I remember being invited as a consultant to help a very large urban congregation in a visioning process for its future. Although it was large, its membership was rapidly aging, and the incoming ripple of new members was no match for its membership decline due to aging and death. They were, rightfully, concerned about their future as a congregation. I met regularly with their core group of 50 or so leaders for several months. Together we attempted to diagnose the realities of the congregation and search for direction for the future.

I asked them to think about what the city would miss if their congregation was no longer active. They listed a whole variety of programs and initiatives that were active in the congregation. I asked them to think about anything the congregation was offering that was not also being offered by the synagogue, the mosque, governmental agencies, the public school, or the community centre. After a significant time of discernment and scrutiny, they could not think of a single thing that they were offering that other faiths or governmental social services were not also offering. I asked about "value added" in terms of the church's involvement. They couldn't think of anything.

I gently tried to steer them toward thinking of the nature of the church – as a community of Jesus' understanding of the kingdom present, and so on. Nothing came to mind. I got a bit more aggressive and began to suggest that if what they are offering is done better by others, perhaps they should consider closing and designating their still-substantial budgets to partner with these other groups, thus avoiding duplication. They would not hear of such a suggestion. It seemed insulting to them. Finally, after much soul-searching, they suggested that their congregation, as a church of Christ, was indeed offering two things that no one else was: one was maintaining the German language for their services, the other was four-part harmony singing. It took several sessions more until one of them said, "Well, Jesus is pretty central to our understandings, which is not so true in the mosque, the synagogue, or the social service departments." Aha! That generated a breakthrough that allowed for another whole area of consideration to open up for planning the future.

What had happened? This congregation was rapidly approaching its 100th birthday. In the process of aging, it had forgotten who it was. When they were reminded, they became excited. How strange that it is possible to forget or overlook our basic identity.

Is it any wonder that a common complaint about "church" is that it is too restrictive in its agenda, too limiting in its imagination, too colonial in its practice, too imposing in its faith, too doctrinally rigid and insensitive in its belief, or too socially conservative to be useful?

In short, the church is too uninspiring to many who are interested in exploring a potential connection.

I have demonstrated – I hope – that a lack of inspiration is not because there is such a ho-hum vision for the church in the biblical witness. On the contrary, the vision articulated there is overwhelming, exploding every category. But it has been domesticated. We must take care not to throw out the vision because of the reality – the baby with the bathwater. The answer lies in renewing our understanding of what is proposed as a biblical vision for being the church and keep moving – plodding if you wish – toward that vision.

Perhaps a modern parable might help to focus our dilemma:

Cancer has devastated the lives of millions around the world. Apparently, there is no cure; nor is there a vaccine. Imagine that one day there is good news. A group of scientists have rediscovered an old, lost or discarded, yet highly effective, treatment for all forms of cancer. They test it anew. It works. It is available. But doctors, medical professionals, politicians, governments, and social agencies refuse to utilize this treatment as a backbone for their cancer care. They continue to use every other technique, drug, and medical procedure but do not incorporate the newly rediscovered treatment into their arsenal of professional processes.

Sometimes I wonder if the banishment of a significant sense of church is akin to this parable. The biblical witness seems to indicate clearly, from Genesis to Revelation, that the preferred strategy of God to reconcile the world to its Creator, to himself, and to his intended purposes is via the formation of alternative communities. Such communities will be the vanguard of God's intentions best understood in the life, teachings, death, and resurrection of Jesus of Nazareth. Yet, we use every strategy under the sun but largely ignore the one that is the leading contender in the biblical message. It is strange indeed.

To summarize:

We need to understand how profoundly God wishes to restore and reconcile all of creation to its intended purposes.

We need to acknowledge that the authority of God to achieve this purpose is emerging in the world (the kingdom of God is coming), and God's solidarity with us invites us into full participation in this process of reconciliation.

As Christians, we look to Jesus to understand more fully how this emerging authority is to function and what it looks like when it enters the realms of creation that do not understand.

Jesus demonstrates – again – that the first priority of kingdom living is that it must be done in community. Thus, the peoplehood of God becomes a preferred vehicle of solidarity for the healing of creation.

The life of this community is both a living witness to the message of reconciliation that it proclaims and the vehicle to make it known to others.

This is indeed very good news. It is gospel.

Afterwords

Janet Plenert:

Drawing on the African concept of *ubuntu* ("I am because you are"), Archbishop Desmond Tutu said, "You can't exist as a human being in isolation." In this marvellous yet challenging little book, Suderman takes that the next step further. Not only can we not be human in isolation, but the joining together of individual humans into a peoplehood is at the core of God's plan to redeem and restore the world.

Suderman skillfully draws us from Genesis through Revelation, showing how God is forming a peoplehood and how this peoplehood is the central strategy of God for the restoration of the world to its original intentions. The image is a beautiful one of all tribes, nations, peoples, and languages coming together to worship and serve God.

(see Rev 7:9)

In today's world however, we seem to be splintering rather than joining together. We are suspicious (overtly or subconsciously) of those different than ourselves. We gather in cultural enclaves. Political parties lure us to define ourselves as being one side or the other. We split churches into more like-minded groupings. We allow racism to go unchallenged or gloss the surface of it by ignoring the roots that anchor it in our society.

To take seriously God's strategy of building a people who are the agents of God's divine mission, today's church must embrace and face this call more boldly, more overtly, and with more humility. We may be just a little toe or toenail in the larger Body. But to place our allegiance and best energy into a gathering of little toes that disrespect the other body parts does not help us fulfill our role in the whole Body. At the very least, for the church to be the church, every part of the church needs to step back in humility and recognize that we are but a microscopic portion of the whole Body. And it does us no good for one part of the Body to attack another.

In my context of early 21st century Canadian church, there is skepticism about the "institutional church." Many church denominational structures are in decline. Organizational loyalty for church programs and agencies continues strong among older demographics, but the same is not true of younger generations. Suderman has a refreshing take on institution. I recall lunchroom conversations where he used to say, "If something is worth doing, it is worth institutionalizing."

Institutions are ways of ensuring that good things can be repeated. In North America, we are quick to create formal institutions. We register with the government, follow human resource law, and apply all the needed checks and balances. We would do well to reconsider Suderman's point and simplify our thinking. Good institutions are designed to ensure that good things can be repeated. And for this to happen, we need to know what the good things are that need repeating! As obvious as it sounds, it is often the case that "institutional" members forget – or have never been taught – the foundational "good" they are called to accomplish – be it a national denomination or an ad hoc local church committee. The church must know, and be ready to articulate, the good news for which it exists!

Solidarity. Such a strong word. It conjures ideas of linked arms, strong bonds of support, like-mindedness, cohesion, and fierce camaraderie. Suderman shows through Bible examination how Jesus is in solidarity with his community of disciples, how God is in solidarity with Jesus, and therefore how God is in solidarity with humans. God can be enfleshed in the human community. Pause. Breathtaking indeed! The mission and authority of Jesus becomes the mission and authority of the disciples.

The people that God is raising up are divine agents called to live into and bring about the restored world.

This is not only awe inspiring, it is terrifying and exhilarating! How would we carry ourselves differently if we, well, "incarnated" this reality more fully? Would we each be more generous, gentle, loving, patient, and kind in our words and actions? Would we be bolder, angrier, and more direct in our naming injustice, calling out racism, and acting against oppression? Would we as communities of faith spend our energy differently? Would we work harder at loving our enemies by keeping them closer and listening to them more deeply? What difference would it make if we took this solidarity/enfleshment more seriously?

Suderman's study of Ephesians 6 and getting dressed in the armour of God is instructive. The tools in our toolkit, which we need to live among the weeds and face the evil powers, are truth, justice, the gospel of peace, faith, salvation, the word of God, prayer, and perseverance. Suderman briefly points out that tools such as vengeance and fury are left out. We would do well to reflect anew and in depth on this. Also left out of our toolkit are self-righteousness, judgment, pride, aggression, and oppression. While the church has reconsidered some of its once-defended tenets toward issues such as slavery and the equality of women, many Christians and churches continue to back racist and misogynous political leaders, send their young people into war, support the death penalty, and remain silent in the face of police brutality and other injustices. It would seem that a deep study of this might cause us to remove some armour that is not ours to wear, while trying on pieces we have sometimes ignored.

In so doing, I suspect we might, by necessity, become radical agents dismantling evils in our society.

Suderman gently describes a cosmic vision for the church. It is simple, yet never simplistic. It is aspirational, inspirational, and invitational. We need not throw the baby (the church) out with the bathwater. But we will need to tend it day after day as we struggle to clear the debris in the path of its profound purpose.

Janet Plenert, MATS, lives with her family in Winnipeg where she is active in her home congregation and in volunteer roles for the broader church. Formerly she worked on the Executive Staff of Mennonite Church Canada and as Director of Mennonite Disaster Service Canada. She also served as Vice-President of Mennonite World Conference.

Cynthia Peacock:

It is a privilege for me to respond briefly to this helpful focus on the life of the church. I have learned to appreciate Robert and Irene's teaching presence in their several assignments in India and in our joint work with Mennonite World Conference. They came to us with humility, experience, and knowledge. Robert's exposure to the church in many countries is a source of help and inspiration to us all.

This book asks us to re-look, re-think, and re-do the role of the church in the midst of the evil and hopelessness of the world. What steps can we take to be active co-workers with God in God's desire for reconciliation, peace, and justice?

I like the adage of "the baby and the bathwater." It is absolutely relevant to what I see in the life of our churches. Fundamentalism often blinds us to the beauty of God's kingdom present in the world. Suderman's insights into the parable of the wheat and the weeds are especially helpful in the Indian/Asian context where Christians live as a small minority religious group. It is a privilege to be a minority because it gives us an opportunity to be a Sermon on the Mount witness to the majority. We need to take good care of this "baby."

The parable of the wheat and the weeds is very important in my Indian context and speaks to various issues we face as a church in India. While we have often been taught to "separate" from the world, this parable teaches us that the wheat and the weeds are meant to grow up together in the same world. There is much in our culture, our traditions, and our ways of being that should be incorporated into our understandings of being a new and alternative community in Christ for the world. We are asked to watch out, but not to do away with the good found in our culture and traditions. Our task is not to uproot what is around us, but to demonstrate another alternative to our culture. We mingle with and do not separate from the cultures around us. The new community is called to be visible, not hidden. This book helps us to re-think and re-do this radical separation between church and world that we have often taken for granted. This call for visibility is a significant, but welcome, challenge to our churches.

The focus of this book also helps us understand more fully our responsibilities of relating to other denominations. Rather than see each other as competitors or as errant, we can see each other as focusing on different parts of the 96 images that are highlighted in the New Testament. These images are not meant to cause division in the body of Christ. They are meant to broaden the impact of the Christian presence in our culture. They are not obstacles to relationships. They are opportunities to learn, share, and grow together. Such reciprocal abiding in love will strengthen us and allow us to function better as salt and light in our context and in the global context. These are opportunities of God. They are not threats or disagreements.

Another helpful focus of the book is the reminder that the solidarity between Jesus and his followers includes the authority to forgive each other. We need to hear that. Too often instead of a spirit of forgiveness, we have developed a spirit of critique, challenge, and noncooperation. The humility needed to be able to forgive as Christ forgave is an important lesson for us. It will strengthen our witness to those around us and with each other. Our diversity can be a signal of unity and generate solidarity rather than division among us. This sends a very positive and lasting signal that unity is possible in the midst of diversity and that hearts can be changed by the power of God.

This book also helpfully points to the vocation of the church as teacher. This too is an important challenge that we need to re-think. The idea that the teaching and example of the church has the capacity to make the powers tremble is a significant focus that we need to take more seriously – both in our own and in the global context. In learning to do this better, the church becomes a source of hope in and for the world.

In summary, this book is profound. It challenges our context. It is mind-stretching and thought-provoking. It can help us to re-focus many things as we struggle to be faithful to God in our context – with those not in the church, and with those in churches that are not our own. I do hope this book will receive very broad, ecumenical exposure. May God help us all to be the church in this time.

Cynthia Peacock lives in Kolkata, India. She is an active church leader. She is a long-time worker with Mennonite Central Committee India and Mennonite Christian Service Fellowship of India, and more recently works as the regional representative in India for Mennonite World Conference. She is also the former chair of the Deacons Commission of MWC.

Moses Falco:

For a number of years, I've been wrestling with the question: What difference does the gospel of Jesus Christ actually make in our world? As a follower of Jesus, I've been swept up into the story of God and overwhelmed by the love and grace I experience through my adoption into God's family. However, as a pastor I've struggled to reconcile the invasion of God's kingdom in the world with the constant violence, hate, greed, abuse, and injustice I see all around me.

If there is a God, and *if* Jesus is the truest revelation we have of who that God is, and *if* the way of Jesus does really lead to life, then you might expect that those who follow after Jesus would also embody and reflect the character of their Creator. And herein lies the very issue that Robert Suderman tackles in his book: that the inconsistencies between the gospel and those who claim to live it out have turned people away from belonging to that body – the Church.

As I read and wrestled with Suderman's ecclesiology, I began to realize that my initial question is the kind that allows us to throw out the baby with the bathwater. We've come to a place in our collective spirituality (at least for the North American Church) where we're able to separate the message of Jesus from the mission of the Church. We can ask what difference the gospel of Jesus makes in the world without including the body of Christ in the answer, as if we can get rid of the Church and still have Jesus.

That's why this book is so important. Suderman reminds the Church of several things we are in danger of forgetting. First, that the Church belongs to God and stands in continuity with how God has worked in this world from the beginning. Second, that it is through the Church that God is working to accomplish God's reconciliation plan in the world. And lastly, that the Church is the Church only when it is rooted (intertwined) in Jesus Christ, thereby equipping it to live as a community of hope.

As revolutionary as this kind of ecclesiology is, I realize that it is also offensive because it shakes and challenges us in ways we don't always appreciate. Those who are steeped in institutional Christianity are confronted with the idea that Church isn't something we go to, watch, shop around for, or own; it's something what we *are*. And those who have come to think that they can have Jesus without belonging to the Church must have their imagination reignited to realize that those who follow Jesus, of any race, nationality, gender, ability, and sexuality, as well as both past and present, *are* the Church.

The challenge for pastors, like me, is how to actualize this ecclesiological vision in a local congregation. How do we invite people to belong to a community of believers in such a way that doesn't scare them away yet takes the responsibility of belonging to the Church seriously? How do we inspire those who grew up in a church to be open to the diversity of the global people of God? How do we come to terms with the wrongs the Church has done? How do we inspire our communities to embrace the grand vision of God's Church, as Suderman challenges us to?

I sense some changes on the horizon for the North American Church, which I believe will allow us to live out our ecclesiology more faithfully. I think we will hold our institutions more loosely, prioritizing people over programs and opening ourselves up to welcome people into genuine community. I also think we will continue to equip the priesthood of all believers rather than relying on professionals, recognizing that the ministry of the Church is not for Christians to receive but to participate in. I also believe we will focus on our mission rather than our individual needs, reaching out wider than our local church communities and risking discomfort for the sake of God's kingdom.

As I continue to wrestle with what it means to be the Church, I am starting to change my original question to ask the kind of question Suderman asked: What difference does the Church actually make in our community, country, or world? Asking this question will force us to constantly have our ecclesiology front and centre. And what I've come to realize is that this question is not so different from my first question: What difference does the gospel make? In fact, the more time I spend in the Church, the more indistinguishable these questions become.

The reason I'm still a part of the Church is because I'm convinced that the answers to these questions are "yes!" I see the difference the Church makes in how people of all walks of life are welcomed into a new family and invited to reorient their lives around the lordship of Jesus. I see it in the way Christians give up of their wealth in order to care for those within their community who are struggling. I see it in the ways the Church addresses issues of justice such as poverty, climate change, and colonialism. I see it in the Church's advocacy for peace and unity around the world, serving and equipping where it can. Of course the Church doesn't always get it right, but I could go on and on about the ways in which I see God at work in God's people. Yes, the Church makes a difference in this world. And because the Church makes a difference, I am confident that the gospel of Jesus Christ does too.

Moses Falco is a husband, father, and a Mennonite pastor in Winnipeg, Manitoba. He was drawn to the Mennonite tradition because of its focus on peace, community discernment, and the priesthood of all believers. Together with his wife, Jessica, the family loves being part of the Church. He has served as pastor since 2015.

Other Books Published

Calloused Hands, Courageous Souls. Robert J. Suderman: translated by W. Derek Suderman: Monrovia, California: MARC, 1998.

Discipulado Cristiano al Servicio del Reino. Roberto J. Suderman: Ciudad de Guatemala, Guatemala: Ediciones Semilla/CLARA, 1994.

Encounters on the Way: Nourished by Life. Robert J. Suderman: Self-published: Tellwell Talent, 2020.

God's People Now! Face to Face with Mennonite Church Canada. Robert J. Suderman: Waterloo, Ontario: Herald Press, 2007.

Re-Imagining the Church: Implications of Being a People in the World. Robert J. Suderman: edited by Andrew G. Suderman: Eugene, Oregon: Wipf and Stock, 2016.

Tengan Valor: Yo he Vencido al Mundo. Roberto J. Suderman: Ciudad de Guatemala, Guatemala: Ediciones Semilla/CLARA, MARC, 1998.

The Replacement Pattern in the Fourth Gospel: A Persecuted Community Confronts Its Past. Robert J. Suderman: Bogotá, Colombia: La Pontificia Universidad Javeriana, 1994.

What Others Are Saying

The Baby and the Bathwater is a precious little book that will do a least three things for you. First, it will show you that the obituaries of the church have been premature. Second, it will take you on a breathtaking Bible journey to recover God's vision for the church today. And third, it will convince you that despite the grandeur of his plan of reconciliation, God has always done it through incarnation. He is counting on the flesh-and-blood communities that make up his people in this world, however imperfect.

- Erich Baumgartner, PhD, Professor of Intercultural Studies, Andrews University, Seventh-day Adventist.

Why bother with the church? For many in the 21st century, the church is not a problem to be solved, it's simply not interesting or relevant. With keen biblical insight, Suderman lifts our eyes to the horizon to God's urgent call and cosmic purpose for the assembled community of Christ's disciples. God has imagined the church as both "demonstration and vehicle" of a peoplehood moving from Eden to the New Jerusalem. Here is a compelling and aspirational vision for such a time as this.

- David Boshart, PhD, President of Anabaptist Mennonite Biblical Seminary.

At a time when the mainline Protestant church is in decline and suffering from a public critique of its institutional nature, Dr. Robert Suderman calls the church to reclaim its mission and to truly understand the purpose of its structure, which by form and calling is institutional. Biblically grounded and infused with years of engaged service throughout the world, Suderman reminds readers of the many images used by the biblical writers to describe the work of the church, while pointing to the particular use of ekklesia or "called out" to define the first church's understanding of its mission. Written in an accessible manner, readers are drawn beyond stale categories to see the fullness of the church's calling and invited to reengage the church's mission as we live, worship, and work between Eden and the New Jerusalem.

- Jeff Carpenter, D.Min, President of Bethany Seminary, Church of the Brethren.

Biblically rooted, theologically innovative, and ethically pertinent, Dr. Suderman presents a compelling case for reclaiming centrality for ecclesiology in Christian theology. Going beyond the conventional contours of ecclesiological discourse, he instills fresh life and dynamism into the debate. He does this by interpreting the nature and vocation of the Church primarily in terms of "formation of new peoplehood in history," thus offering a life-centric, cosmic, and holistic ecclesiology. This is much needed new thinking, which I am sure will prompt fresh interest in the doctrine of the Church.

- Metropolitan Dr. Geevarghese Coorilos, Syriac Orthodox Church, India; Moderator, World Council of Churches Commission on World Mission and Evangelism.

In this book, Suderman draws upon his half-century of ecclesial experience to re-cast a Kingdom-centered vision of the church that is worthy of the cosmic significance for which God designed it. There is no naïve panacea here. Suderman faces head-on the checkered history and the current challenges of the church. Nonetheless, poised as we are at the edge of a crumbling Christendom, Suderman's retrieval from the past points the way forward for a Jesus-centered, missionally-focused expression of the church, a church equipped for the future to which it has been called. Highly recommended!

- Paul Rhodes Eddy, PhD, Professor of Biblical &Theological Studies, Bethel University, and Teaching Pastor, Woodland Hills Church.

How does one measure the fullness of life or the church's fidelity to its vocation? These and other probing questions (and some answers!) make up Suderman's rich text. Through careful analysis of biblical passages interwoven with church history and anecdotes, the author guides the reader to consider how lessons from the past can both inform and transform our theology and practice of being faithful, contextual, Christian communities in this tumultuous 21st century. This book will be a great asset to undergraduate and seminary courses, as well as to home groups and Christians of many traditions seeking better ways to be, in the language of the Apostle Paul, "stars that shine in the darkness" (cf. Phil. 2:15).

- Dr. Rosalee Velloso Ewell, Director of Church Relations, United Bible Societies, England.

Dr. Suderman's *The Baby and the Bathwater* is a wonderful work of theology that warns us against the marginalizing of the church. Simple but profound, direct, to the point, yet personable at the same time, it is an urgent clarion call to Christians everywhere to be the church in these most precarious of times. Like having a conversation with a saint, reading Suderman for me was a gift of much wisdom and scholarship. I deeply appreciate this book!

- David Fitch, PhD, Professor of Evangelical Theology, Northern Seminary.

In *The Baby and the Bathwater*, Robert Suderman gently, compellingly, and succinctly teaches and inspires all who care and wonder about the Church. He engages with current questions about the Christian community with refreshing insights, deeply rooted in the Bible and in the widest Christian tradition. Writing from Anabaptist perspectives, Suderman's ecclesiological vision merits a wide ecumenical consideration. It is a gift to the whole Church.

- The Rev'd Canon Dr. John Gibaut, Anglican Church of Canada, President of Thorneloe University, Sudbury, and former Director of the Commission on Faith and Order, World Council of Churches.

The wisdom of Robert Suderman never ceases to amaze me. The imagery painted by his words gives me hope for the future church. We can make room for something new to begin without destroying the foundations of the past. I encourage both current and future leaders to pick up and study *The Baby and the Bathwater*. The book challenges us all to be Ambassadors of reconciliation as we work through the storms of life and leadership in this God-ordained community we call church.

> *- Glen A. Guyton, M.Ed, Executive Director: Mennonite Church USA.*

Based on his extensive experience in the church, Dr. Suderman writes, "it is evident that an overt, robust, and profound sense of the church's vocation has largely vanished from our vision." It would be difficult to disagree with this analysis. In this short manuscript he lays out the biblical vision of the church in a way that is clear and inspiring. At one point, as he contemplates God's vision for the church, Suderman observes, "If this does not give us goosebumps, we are numbed, apathetic zombies." Study of this manuscript is an antidote to zombie apathy, as we are inspired by God's amazing plan for the church.

> *- Nathan Hoppe, PhD candidate, Orthodox Church of Albania Missionary; Lecturer Logos University, Tirana, Albania.*

While Christian communities often reflect visions that are attentive to boundaries and limitations, Suderman's work highlights the importance of the church as a community of hope in a broken world. Grounded in biblical studies, this volume energetically lays out a multivalent, dynamic, and cosmic vision.

> *- Dr. Karl Koop, Professor of History and Theology, and Director of the Graduate School of Theology and Ministry at Canadian Mennonite University.*

Raise your eyes above any malaise and division in the church today, and consider what Robert Suderman sees from Genesis to Revelation: God wants to use a *people* — the imperfect, struggling, much-criticized church — as God's instrument to restore a broken world. This ambitious agenda is God's work, but it requires human-led structure and organization. Informed by decades of local and cross-cultural church leadership, Suderman draws from Old and New Testaments to project an awesome biblical vision of the church. God calls us to join in restoring all creation – from the natural world to societies and the sinful human heart. Congregations and pastors who catch this huge vision will never be the same.

> *- J. Nelson Kraybill, PhD, President, Mennonite World Conference.*

This exciting book opens up fresh biblical perspectives on being "church" with a provocative question: Do current conceptions of church actually fit the biblical witness? Suderman captures our imagination with a dynamic analysis of church in the New Testament, an analysis that challenges the whole ecumenical movement to self-critical examination of its definition of church and the urgency of reconciliation, as God's plan for all creation.

> *- Prof. Dr. Dirk G. Lange, Assistant General Secretary for Ecumenical Relations, The Lutheran World Federation.*

I commend this Mennonite reflection on "the nature and vocation of the church in light of 21st century realities." Its scope converges with one of the most important contributions of the modern ecumenical movement to contemporary Christianity often impoverished by individualism, namely, to proclaim the centrality of the *Una Sancta* in God's saving design fully revealed in Christ and to call the divided churches to manifest the One Church in active anticipation of the reign to come. We can only do that if we are convinced, as this book contends, of the importance of the church in what the author calls "God's dream for the world," and if we are ready to respond to the call "to reconcile the world to what it can be."

> *- Revd. Dr. Odair Pedroso Mateus, Reformed Church, Director of World Council of Churches Faith and Order Commission and the WCC Bossey Ecumenical Institute.*

If the Church is the baby, it has been centuries since Anabaptist-Mennonites began to neglect the "universal" baby. Now, according to Suderman, it seems we are in danger of throwing out the "local" baby, too. Robert Suderman's life journey has taken him through both the global and the local church. This troubling and inspiring book calls us to recover both. May we heed the summons!

> *- Larry Miller, PhD, Mennonite World Conference General Secretary, 1990-2011; Global Christian Forum Secretary, 2012-2018.*

Imagine the church as an agent of Jesus' prayer: *thy kingdom come; thy will be done on earth.* An agent of hope to the marginalized, the oppressed, the persecuted; amplifying the voices of the poor for the sake of peace and reconciliation. Suderman's sketch of the biblical view of the church's vocation is hope-filled and inspiring.

> - *Joji Pantoja, MESEDEV, Co-founder of the PeaceBuilder's Community, Davao, Philippines; Chair of the Peace Commission of Mennonite World Conference.*

This fascinating title will entice the reader to explore from chapter to chapter, enjoying the observations of this keen observer of things "church-related to kingdom living." This work is a kind of self-reflective critique, both personally and institutionally, on the question of the mission of the church in today's 21st century. Although a Mennonite, Suderman considers other ecclesial realities. His vast pastoral and international experience has enabled him to find ways to objectively look for elements of an ecclesiology of mission and peace. He gently steers communities toward thinking of the nature of the church as a community of Jesus' understanding of the priority of kingdom-living that must be done in community, and this to save "the baby and the bathwater."

- *Dr. James Puglisi, Franciscan Priest and Director, Centro Pro Unione, Rome.*

This is a rich biblical treatment of the Church, ecumenical in spirit, lifting up the Church's continuing central importance in light of Christ. It may be true that the struggles of Christians dealing with the impact of negative forces throughout history have often seemed, in the eyes of many, including some Christians, to diminish the significance and standing of the Church. Still, it would be very difficult, especially for a person of Christian faith, to come away from reading Dr. Suderman's analysis and not be optimistic and enthusiastic about the Church and the witness it gives to the world about the Risen Lord. The story of the Church, as seen in this biblical account, is the story of permanent Hope, the story of Life in Christ, and final victory in Christ.

> - *Monsignor John A. Radano, PhD, Catholic Co-Secretary of the First phase of Mennonite-Catholic International Dialogue 1998-2003.*

Robert Suderman is a passionate advocate for the recovery of a biblical understanding of the church. In a series of thoughtful, easy-to-read reflections, he encourages us to see the ongoing relevancy of God's vision for peoplehood and the impact that might have in our communities today.

- Valerie Rempel, PhD, Vice President and Dean of Fresno Pacific University Biblical Seminary.

Spiritual progress often depends on a shift in perspective on a familiar landscape. Dr. Suderman challenges the Church as a bold institution to embrace all the 96 ways God depicts us, and thus to enter more fully into God's purpose. You will not hear the parable of the wheat and tares or read Ephesians and John's Gospel in the same way again. We are reminded that the Kingdom of God grows alongside the world, transforming it where opportunity arises, and always as the Church being an integral part of God's salvation purpose. God hasn't thrown the baby out with the bathwater; and neither should we.

- Rt. Rev. Alan Scarfe, D.D, Retired Bishop of the Episcopal Diocese of Iowa.

Amid a blizzard of distractions and despair, it is easy to conclude that we have lost our way — and the church has no future. Enter Robert Suderman, a man who knows the ancient, trustworthy paths better than most of us. While it often seems like we've ended up in domesticated dead ends, we could be on a glorious and cosmic adventure, he writes. While we grieve the limitations of church life, the biblical dream for a committed peoplehood is nothing less than the restoration of all creation. With seasoned wisdom, Suderman offers a refreshingly robust call to rediscover how the church, in solidarity with Jesus, can become God's "preferred vehicle for the healing of creation."

- Sara Wenger Shenk, Ed.D, AMBS President Emeritus.

Among the many valuable conversations taking place today about kingdom and collaboration, we are sometimes at risk of forgetting the important role of the Church. Dr. Suderman's newest text reminds us of the biblical call that the Church must remain an active part of these conversations. Not only because we need the reminder (which we do) but also because the Bible requires us to not lose focus on the theological, historical, and biblical role the Church plays in restoring what was lost in the Garden of Eden.

- Brent Sleasman, PhD, President, Winebrenner Seminary, Churches of God General Conference.

Robert Suderman provides a biblical, exegetical understanding of the nature of the Church. His analysis of the life of the Church reveals the tension that the Church experiences: a community in the world without being of the world. This book invites us to reform our communities to constantly play our role of salt and light in a world where the presence of the Church is indispensable.

- Siaka Traoré, Pasteur à l'Eglise Evangélique Mennonite de Bobo-Dioulasso; Burkina Faso.

About the Author

Robert J. Suderman, Dr.Th., has a long history (over five decades) of work in the church and its varied ministries. This includes teaching, executive administration, international assignments, and pastoral training in more than 30 countries around the world. His ecumenical experience is evident on every page. He writes for the "church," not only for his own denomination.

Before retirement, he served as General Secretary of Mennonite Church Canada. Together with his family, he has lived in five countries. He is fluent in both English and Spanish languages. With Irene, his wife of 55 years, he now enjoys retirement in New Hamburg, Ontario.

Suderman has been a tireless proponent of the church, arguing for its central importance in the biblical witness. In this crisp but substantial study, he proposes to trace "the biblical trajectory and wisdom undergirding the nature and vocation of the church." This is robust and compelling ecclesiology, accessible to all.

About the Illustrator

 Ray Dirks is a renowned international artist and curator. He is passionate about the potential of art as a medium to enhance intercultural/interreligious understanding and profound theological insight. He encourages artists and provides platforms for their work. Having worked in 30 countries, he feels most at home when engaging others in their comfort zones, be it a mud hut, a mosque, an Orthodox church, or a dusty bus.

He was the founding director of the Mennonite Heritage Centre Gallery, a program of Mennonite Church Canada (1998). Dirks received the *Above and Beyond for the Arts Award* from the Manitoba Foundation for the Arts (2002); the *Blazer Distinguished Community Service Award* from Canadian Mennonite University (2008); and the *Manitoba Lieutenant Governor's Award for Advancement of Interreligious Understanding* (2018). His *Along the Road to Freedom* exhibition has recently been exhibited in Canada and the USA with some 20 stops.

Together with his wife Katie, Dirks is enjoying retirement in Winnipeg.

www.ingramcontent.com/pod-product-compliance
Lightning Source LLC
LaVergne TN
LVHW011725060526
838200LV00051B/3032